TEAM STUDIES
RELENTLESS

Rod Handley and Gordon Thiessen

ISBN 978-1-938254-08-6

Cross Training Publishing
www.crosstrainingpublishing.com
(308) 293-3891

Library of Congress Cataloging in Publication Data in Progress.

D1316433

I am a Christian first and last.
I am created in the likeness of God Almighty to bring Him glory.
I am a member of Team Jesus Christ. I wear the colors of the cross.

I am a Competitor now and forever. I am made to strain, to stretch and
to succeed in the arena of competition. I am a Christian Competitor
and as such, I face my challenger with the face of Christ.

I do not trust in myself, I do not boast in my abilities or believe in
my own strength. I rely solely on the power of God. I compete for
the pleasure of my Heavenly Father, the honor of Christ and
the reputation of the Holy Spirit.

My attitude on and off the field is above reproach – my conduct beyond criticism.
Whether I am preparing, practicing or playing: I submit to God's authority
and those He has put over me. I respect my coaches, officials, teammates,
and competitors out of respect for the Lord.

My body is the temple of Jesus Christ. I protect it from within and without.
Nothing enters my body that does not honor the Living God.
My sweat is an offering to my Master. My soreness is a sacrifice to my Savior.

I give my all – all of the time. I do not give up.
I do not give in. I do not give out. I am the Lord's warrior – a competitor by conviction
and a disciple of determination.
I am confident beyond reason because my confidence lives in Christ.
The results of my efforts must result in His glory.

Let the competition begin. Let the glory be God's.

Sign the Creed @ www. fca.org

FELLOWSHIP OF
CHRISTIAN ATHLETES

CONTENTS

CONTACTING
THE AUTHORS

Rod Handley
Character That Counts
512 NE Victoria Drive
Lee's Summit, MO 64086
www.characterthatcounts.org

Gordon Thiessen
Cross Training Publishing
15418 Weir Street #177
Omaha, NE 68137
www.crosstrainingpublishing.com

To contact FCA or order FCAGear
call 1-800-289-0909 or
check us out on the web at FCA.org

Team Studies on Character Volume 1, 2, 3, 4, 5, 6, 7
are also available as well as an expanded edition,
Character that Counts for Athletes Volume 1, 2, 3
Team Studies: Gamechanger
Team Studies: In the Zone
Team Studies: Relentless

PREFACE

How do I use this book? This book is designed to help you and your teammates build your character. In FCA we call this type of discussion a Team Bible Study. It is important that you take enough time during your meetings (approximately 29-40 minutes) to go through each section of the study. Each week you will have the opportunity to talk about how you were able to build your character since the previous Team Bible Study. After this time of catching up, you will do a warm up to introduce this week's character trait. This will include a team building exercise. If you have time you could do this as a group. You might even suggest to your coach your whole team could do this outside of the Team Bible Study. After this warm up you will have the opportunity to look into the ultimate source of character building—the Bible—and discover how it might guide you as you build your character.

What is a Team Survey? You will find an optional survey on page 81-82 that you can use with your group either before or after this study.

What is the Practice Evaluation Form? This can be used as an accountability tool for applying the lessons from this book (page 83).

What is a Team Bible Study? A Team Bible Study is a group of athletes from a team desiring to discuss real life and build their character through God's principles.

How big should a Team Bible Study be? This is hard to say, but generally people feel most comfortable talking and learning in a group of 10 or fewer. The bottom line is that those on your team who want to be involved should have the chance, if it is only 3 or even if it is over 20.

When should we meet? Team Bible Study groups typically meet during the team's season. The best time to do it is before or after practice, so you are not adding another time commitment to your already busy life.

How can I get the most out of this? You will get out of this exactly what you put into it. How honest you are with yourself and the others in the group will determine how much you will get out of this. It might be a stretch for some of you to risk being vulnerable for the first time.

Who can lead a Team Bible Study? Team Bible Studies are best led by someone connected with your team! It could be a player, coach, assistant coach, chaplain, etc. It is not difficult to lead a Team Bible Study. You don't have to be an expert in any particular area. It is important that Team Bible Study leaders are aware of FCA's Statement of Faith and are in agreement with it.

What is the Gospel? Christians often say that Jesus died for our sins. But what does that mean? Why did He die? What has He accomplished by His death on the cross? What effect does His death on a cross have on us? With this book, we have selected key themes that focus on the Gospel with each character trait. However, to be clear, here are the Gospel facts you should repeatedly review with your students.

Gospel Facts: That the one and only one God, who is holy, made us in His image to know Him. However, we have sinned and cut ourselves off from Him. Because of God's love for us, God became a man in Jesus, lived a perfect life, and died on the cross. He fulfilled the law Himself by taking on the punishment we deserved for the sins of all those who ever turn to and trust Him. He rose again from the dead, showing that God accepted Christ's sacrifice and that God's wrath against us had been exhausted. Now, God calls us to repent of our sins and trust in Christ, we are born again into a new life, an eternal life with God.

FCA's Team Bible Study Commitments

- Priority--As long as you are a part of the Team Bible Study, you must make the meetings a priority.
- Participation--Everyone participates, no one dominates.
- Respect--Everyone is given the right to his own opinion, and all questions are encouraged and respected.
- Confidentiality--Anything that is said in the group stays in the group and is never repeated outside of the meeting.
- Empty Chair--The group remains open to new teammates.
- Support--Permission is given to call upon each other in times of need--even in the middle of the night.
- Giving Advice--Unsolicited advice is not allowed.
- Multiplication--We agree to do everything in our power to pray that others on your team would be interested in developing their character through God's principles.

LOVE

GOD PURSUES ME

"Only goodness and faithful love will pursue me all the days of my life..." Psalm 23:6

It feels good to be wanted. From the playground to the pros, top athletes are pursued to make the team better. But those pursuits are based on what we as individuals can do rather than who we are on the inside. Too often, once we have nothing else to offer or our talents and abilities are diminished, those who pursued us because of external qualities are suddenly less interested in continuing the relationship.

That's what makes God's love for us so remarkable. It's not based on our physical appearance, talents, how good of a person we are or any good things that we have done. The fact of the matter is we can never be good enough for God's love, yet as David wrote in Psalm 23:6, He pursues us all the days of our lives. It's true. More than anything, God wants a deep, meaningful relationship with you!

Love: Having a deep personal attachment and affection for another person.

1. Share a time when someone loved you deeply. How did you feel?
2. Complete this sentence: I feel loved when _____.

Team Builder: Everyone spread out in an open area. When the leader yells "Everybody's it!" start running around trying to tag the others while avoiding getting tagged. If you get tagged, sit down, extend your arms and try to tag those left running around. If two people tag each other at the same time, both must sit down. Keep this up until one player is left standing. (1) What was more enjoyable, pursuing the other players or being pursued? (2) Did you feel love during this game?

When Brittany Viola qualified for the 2012 Olympics, it was the culmination of a long journey complete with serious highs and lows. But the platform diver says it was a serious battle with bulimia in 2006 that caused her to come face to face with her greatest struggle yet. While at an eating disorder facility in Arizona, Viola accepted Christ as her Savior, but once back at the University of Miami, she began to struggle again. That's when a teammate shared the truth of God's love with her and she was able to understand the power and truth found in these words written by David in Psalm 139:13-16.

Brittany shares, "There was light shining in times of darkness. As I continued to struggle with my eating disorder, I would be reminded that God still loved me even when I did not love myself. His forgiveness helped me to forgive myself. His truth allowed me to replace the many lies in my head. He saw me as fearfully and wonderfully made, His perfect creation, chosen, holy, and dearly loved."

In Luke 19:1-10, we find a story of pursuit in a man named Zacchaeus. There was nothing special about Zacchaeus. In fact,

he was despised by almost everyone who knew him. That's because Zacchaeus was a Jewish man working for the Roman Empire as a tax collector. At best, he was considered a loathsome cheat. At worst, he was viewed as a traitor against his own people.

However, when Jesus passed through his town, Zacchaeus wanted to catch a glimpse of this man that everyone was talking about. He was described as a short man, so in order to see over the crowd, he climbed a tree for a better view. When Jesus came by, He looked up at Zacchaeus and said, "Hurry and come down because today I must stay at your house." (v. 5)

Of all the people Jesus could have pursued, Zacchaeus was among the least likely candidates. This astonished the people around and some even began to complain. "He's gone to lodge with a sinful man!" (v. 6)

Zacchaeus was so moved by Jesus' unconditional love that he repented of sins right there and vowed to pay four times what he owed anyone he had cheated and give half of his wealth to the poor. Jesus responded by forgiving Zacchaeus of his sins and then spending time with him in his home.

1. Can you describe a dark time in your life?

2. Did you feel God's love during that experience? Explain.

3. Why do you think Zacchaeus wanted to see Jesus so badly?

4. Why do you think that Jesus' display of love had such an profound impact on Zacchaeus?

WRAPUP

In these two stories, you've read about how God's relentless love changed two lives. Take some time to share some of your story and how God's love has changed your life.

1. Can you relate to either of these two stories (Brittany Viola or Zacchaeus)? How so?

2. Do you ever struggle to embrace God's love for you? If so, why do you think that's the case?

Spiritual Training Points

• **God's Love Is Unconditional:** God's love is not based on performance. Nothing will make God love you any less or any more than He already does. Read Isaiah 54:10.

• **God's Love Is For Everyone:** God doesn't love one person more than another. He loves you because you are His creation. Read Psalm 139:13-16.

• **God's Love Is Forever:** Because God is infinite, His love has no end. God's love is bottomless! Read 1 John 4:16. In John 15:13, the Bible says, "No one has greater love than this, that someone would lay down his life for his friends."

3. How would this ancient statement apply to your team dynamic?

4. Do you think that the more love there is on a team, the greater effort and teamwork? Or is it more important for everyone to be tough? Why?

Any serious team has one goal in mind: to win the prize. The relentless pursuit of the championship, trophy or medal drives the competitor to practice and play with an intense focus and determination in order to obtain the ultimate reward. Passion drives them to reach that goal. But God too has a prize that He is pursuing. And that prize is you. That's exactly why Jesus died on the cross in order to pay for our sin (John 3:16-17 and Romans 5:8).

God will never force you to accept His love. He offers it to you and then allows you to make the choice—receive it or keep running from it. Until then, He will relentlessly pursue you and a real relationship with you.

How to have a relationship with Jesus and understanding the Gospel can be found on page 6. The FCA "More Than Winning" tract is also a great resource for understanding the Good News.

If you have already made that commitment, ask God to reveal those areas in your life where you still need God's love to bring healing and understanding. Ask the Lord for guidance to help you as you begin your own relentless pursuit of Him.

RELENTLESS

Review the Spiritual Training Points discussed earlier. Prayerfully ask God to reveal His love to you. As you begin to receive and understand God's love for you, write down how His love changes you and how it will continue to impact you in the future.

DEVOTION

"Love the Lord your God with all your heart, with all your soul, and with all your strength." Deut. 6:5

When Ryan Hall was 14 years old, he felt inspired to run around the lake one afternoon—and he's been running ever since. On that day, Hall says God was literally calling him to be one of the best runners in the world, and now, he is the fastest American-born marathoner and a two-time Olympian.

During his college days at Stanford, however, failure and frustration caused him to give up on running for short time. But it didn't take Hall long to get back on God's path for his life. In fact, it was the memory of that run around the lake as a teenager that reminded him why he runs in the first place. Perhaps that's why one of Hall's favorite Bible verses is all about total and complete devotion to the Lord, from 2 Chronicles 16:9. Now, when Hall trains and competes, He thinks about the fact that God is watching Him and how He is pleased with his effort.

Devotion: Being earnestly and enthusiastically committed to pursuing something of great value.

1. Describe the most difficult drill that your team has participated in?

2. What gave your team the internal drive to stick with it even when it would have been easier to give up?

Team Builder: Have someone in the Huddle demonstrate the drill from the question above, or the Huddle Leader can run the drill while the group participates. Make sure the drill is non-contact to avoid injuries.

Ryan Hall commented, "I hope that my story leads people into an experience with Jesus. I would hope that I inspire people to look to the Heavens for strength and to enter into a relationship with the One who has infinite power and love and who created us to love Him and to be loved by Him."

Every athlete is born with some measure of talent and skill. But it's the level of devotion that separates the good competitors from the great. No athlete, not even the elite ones, can reach his or her full potential without being fully committed to being the best he or she can be. That's why great competitors are relentless in their training, consistent in their efforts at practice, and focused on learning everything they can about their sport. Discipline and devotion are the ultimate keys to personal greatness.

Discipline and devotion are likewise vital tools in the life of a believer. When we enter into a relationship with Jesus, we must be fully committed to knowing Him more every day. Just as an athlete can't expect to get better without targeted training and practice, a Christian can't expect

to grow in his or her relationship with Him unless he or she pursues Him with whole heart, mind and strength. This requires consistent devotion to spiritual disciplines: reading and studying the Bible, prayer and spending time with other Christians.

Many people experienced God's love through the earthly ministry of Jesus, but not all of them surrendered their lives in return. Mary Magdalene, however, was one individual who devoted her very existence to Jesus. In Luke 8:2, we read that Jesus cast seven demons out of Mary. After that radical transformation, she faithfully followed Him, along with the 12 disciples and some other women whom Jesus had healed.

Mary Magdalene's persistent devotion led her to be near Jesus during three pivotal points of Jesus' death and resurrection: (1) She stayed at the Cross along with Jesus' mother when His own disciples abandoned Him out of fear (Mark 15:40); (2) She was at the tomb when Jesus was buried (Mark 15:47); and (3) She was the first one to discover Jesus' empty tomb (John 20:1).

1. On a scale of 1 to 10, how would you rank your team's devotion to pursuing athletic goals? (1 being "not devoted at all" and 10 being "completely devoted")?
2. What are some factors that play a role in how devoted your team is?
3. How is the team dynamic different when the whole team is pursuing an important goal together instead of individuals chasing after things that aren't important?
4. What are some things that tend to distract your team from getting closer to Jesus?
5. Has fear ever kept you from getting closer to Jesus?

Mary Magdalene's devotion to Jesus always kept her close to Him even at times when being close brought scrutiny and potential danger to her and other followers.

Where are you on your pursuit of Jesus Christ? Draw a circular race track with a start and finish line and place an "x" where you see yourself currently on your spiritual journey. Are you just getting started, somewhere on the course, or are you growing closer to Christ every day? By assessing your current situation (just getting started, continuing the course, getting closer to Christ, etc.), you can make the proper adjustments on your spiritual journey.

Spiritual Training Points

• **Read God's Game Plan:** God's Word provides absolute truth and instruction for our life. Read 2 Timothy 3:16-17.

• **Talk To Your Coach:** Prayer is our way to communicate with God and hear from Him. Read Philippians 4:6-7.

• **Build Your Team:** Get involved in a Bible-believing church and surround yourself with Christian friends. Read Hebrews 10:25.

Psalm 63:8 tells us, "I follow close to You; Your right hand holds on to me." As this verse explains, when we closely follow Jesus, we will reap the benefits of His guidance, His protection and His blessing. The relentless pursuit of Christ is marked by joy, not drudgery. We can delight in His Word. We can delight in His life. We can delight in His love. Deuteronomy 6:5 will become a reality in our lives, and we will reach our full potential as believers and begin to live out the truth as noted in Hebrews 10:39, "But we are not those who draw back and are destroyed, but those who have faith and obtain life."

1. How can you further your pursuit of Christ, regardless of where you are on the journey?

2. Who do you know that demonstrates true devotion to Jesus Christ? Is that person another teammate?

3. What is it about that person that shows they are pursuing Christ?

4. Do you think they would be the same without reading the Bible, praying and spending time with other Christians?

5. Draw a table with five category headings. Label two of them Bible Study and Prayer. In each of the three blank columns, put a heading that identifies something that takes up much of your time. Under each heading, write down four or five personal benefits for each category. Discuss with your team and compare the benefits for each. Prayerfully ask God to reveal ways to help you and your team put Bible devotion and prayer as your top priorities.

RELENTLESS

When I was 17 years old, I (Rod) was introduced to a "Quiet Time." This is time alone with God, allowing Him to speak to me through the Bible and communicating with Him through prayer. This intimate devotional time with God is key to deep Christian growth and maturity. Every committed Christian has this discipline as a core priority. Establish, renew and deepen your daily time with God before anything else gets your attention. Be relentless in your pursuit of Him!

FREEDOM

"Christ has liberated us to be free. Stand firm then and don't submit again to a yoke of slavery." Galatians 5:1

When All-Star slugger Josh Hamilton steps into the batter's box, he does so with a sense of freedom and joy. He was the American League MVP in 2010 and tied the MLB record with four home runs in one game during the 2012 season. But just a few years earlier, he almost gave his entire career away in exchange for a life of drugs and alcohol.

During his minor league career, he was suspended for repeatedly violating the league's drug policy. For four years, he battled emotional depression, physical ailment and spiritual oppression. But during his darkest hours, God delivered Hamilton from his addiction through faithful family members and friends, divine encounters with strangers and the comfort and conviction of the Holy Spirit.

Freedom: Experiencing total unrestraint from all areas of bondage.

1. What are some things that might "weigh down" your team or keep them from performing to the best of their ability?
2. What are some "weights" that have slowed down your team's pursuits?

Team Builder: Get a backpack, some heavy objects (i.e. rocks, books, etc.) and a stopwatch. Map out a path for several volunteers to run a timed race. Have them run the distance without the backpack. Then have them run the same path with the backpack and half of the heavy objects. Then have them run it with the backpack and all of the heavy objects. Time each run and compare the different results.

It doesn't take much to stop an athlete from achieving peak performance. Even a minor injury can slow down a pursuit of excellence, while serious injuries and wrong choices can completely derail an athlete from reaching goals and fulfilling dreams.

As we pursue Christ, the consequences of sin and pain can take our focus off of Him and cause us to live a defeated life. But Paul explains in Galatians 5:1 that Jesus died on the Cross and rose from the dead to bring us freedom from our past mistakes and healing from the hurtful things that have been done against us. Through Jesus, we can experience the promises of forgiveness, healing and an abundant life—a life that is marked by supernatural peace and joy, true fulfillment and eternal purpose that transcends the world's definition of success.

U.S. Soccer team member Tobin Heath went through a time when her identity was wrapped up in performance. She grew to understand that there is great freedom in embracing His forgiveness. It's a freedom that allows her to play fearlessly and joyfully. Heath said, "Having Jesus transform your life is a miracle because He takes people that were dead and He brings them back to life...He restores things that I would think could never be fixed...that were just completely broken."

In Mark 2:1-12, there is a story about a paralyzed man who was looking for physical healing but ended up finding something even better. While Jesus was in Capernaum, he went to a home and began teaching a large group of people. There was no room for anyone to get into the house. So when four friends brought the paralyzed man to see Jesus, they went around the crowd, carried the stretcher to the top of the house, tore an opening in the roof and gently lowered the man to Jesus. Some of the religious leaders were there and were offended that Jesus thought He could forgive the man's sins. Even though they didn't say this out loud, Jesus knew what they were thinking and He challenged them in verses 9-11 (read this now). The man did just as Jesus commanded. He got up, picked up his mat and walked home. Not only did he receive spiritual healing from his sins that day, he also received physical healing and was free to live an abundant life in Christ.

1. Read John 10:10. What do you think abundant life should look like for the follower of Christ?

2. To which of these two stories can you best relate? Explain.

3. Why do you think Jesus forgave the man of his sins before He healed him?

 WRAPUP

One of the most powerful expressions of freedom is written in Psalm 51, a prayer by King David after Nathan called him out for committing adultery with another man's wife and then placing that man on the frontline of battle so he would be killed, allowing David to marry the woman. No matter what your sin or hurt is, David's prayer is a relevant tool that can be used in your own personal journey to an abundant life in Christ (read verses 10, 12 and 14).

Saying that prayer—asking for God's forgiveness and genuinely offering forgiveness to others—and then continuing to walk it out in faith will open the door to a new kind of freedom. It will be a freedom that brings the abundant life Christ promises. This freedom will help you bring out the best in your teammates. It will give you the strength to be an example in the locker room. It will give you courage to be an influence on your campus.

In these stories, you've read about the importance of having spiritual freedom. Take some time to share things that have hindered your relationship with Jesus and how you can experience freedom going forward.

Spiritual Training Points

• **Recognize Sins and Hurts In Your Life:** Pray for God to reveal emotional pain and past hurts you've buried inside. Read Psalm 139:23-24.

• **Forgiveness:** There are three different ways to practice forgiveness: (1) Ask for forgiveness from God and others. Put aside pride and admit you have sinned against God and those you have hurt. Read 1 John 1:9. (2) Give forgiveness to those who have hurt you. Forgive others and do not hold a grudge. Unforgiveness can block God's blessings for us. Read Matthew 6:14-15. (3) Receive forgiveness from God, yourself and others. Forgive yourself for past mistakes and bad choices. The conse-quences don't always go away, but forgiveness will always lead to freedom from regret. Truly accept God's forgiveness and the forgiveness of others. Read Romans 8:1-2.

• **Walk in Abundant Life:** Let go of the bitterness and pain of unforgiveness, and you will be healed. You can be freed from fear and anxiety. You can be whole in Jesus Christ. Read 2 Corinthians 3:17.

1. Re-read Galatians 5:1. Name some of the sins or hurts that came to mind when you read through this lesson. How have those things equated to spiritual "slavery" in your life?
2. What freedom would you experience if you would allow Jesus to take away those sins and hurts?
3. What part of forgiveness is most difficult for you: asking for forgiveness, giving forgiveness or receiving forgiveness?
4. Who do you need to forgive or ask for forgiveness on your team? Make a plan right now to speak to this teammate.

RELENTLESS

Personalize David's prayer from Psalm 51 and ask God to examine your heart for unforgiven sin, bitterness or hurts you've been holding on to, and then turn those things over to Him. Make the commitment to release them for good. You also might consider finding a leader with whom you can share your story so they might lift you up in prayer and provide accountability for your commitment to pursuing relentless freedom.

MISSION

I PURSUE OTHERS

"Go into all the world and preach the Gospel to the whole creation." Mark 16:15

The mark of a great athlete is that he or she not only competes to the best of his or her ability but brings out the best in coaches and teammates. As the athlete pursues excellence, his or her example rubs off on others and can even have influence on those watching from a distance.

As Christians, we too have an impact on those closest to us and the people we encounter on a daily basis. God has given each of us a relentless mission to pursue others with the Gospel of Jesus Christ. We are called to love, serve and influence them by exemplifying Christ's character. God compels us to passionately pursue those people He has put in our lives so that they too may experience an abundant life!

Mission: Sharing my life experiences with someone else.

1. What are your views of someone who identifies themselves as a "missionary?"

2. Have you ever considered you are a missionary on your team? Why or why not?

Team Builder:
Before starting, establish boundaries for the game area size. Have two people hold hands and chase the others. Any person they catch joins the chain by linking hands. When another person is caught they can stay together or split into pairs, but they must split into even numbers and can link together at will. This game is played until nobody is left and the entire group is all linked together. Afterward ask these questions: (1) What was more fun—being chased or chasing others? (2) Did expanding the number of chasers make it easier or more difficult to catch people?

Tim Tebow is one of the most polarizing figures in sports, if not within the spectrum of popular culture. Everyone has an opinion about the unorthodox NFL quarterback. Their admiration or dislike for Tebow is based on his unabashed passion for Jesus Christ. He prays on the sidelines. He goes on mission trips. He gives God the glory in all things—win or lose. Some respect his public displays of faith while others take offense to his blending of "religion" and sports.

But Tebow believes that his platform as a professional athlete has been provided in order for him to share the Good News of God's love. Sometimes that means talking with large groups of people. Sometimes it means thanking God in a live interview after a big win. Sometimes it means serving others privately behind the scenes or praying in the locker room with a teammate who is struggling with an injury. Whatever the case, Tebow says that his primary responsibility is to set an example for others, especially his teammates, in word and in action.

Tim states, "You have to work harder than anybody else. When your teammates see that, they are going to respect you and what you say and you are going to have a lot more opportunity to influence them. You also have to be the kind of leader that loves others and tries to encourage them. You've got to care about your teammates on and off the field."

The Apostle Paul, author of several of the New Testament's most influential writings, was a strict Jewish Pharisee who had vigorously persecuted the Christians until a miraculous encounter with God turned him in the opposite direction. From that moment on, he was a changed man and lived only to share the message of God's love with anyone who would listen.

Paul was relentless in his mission to share Christ with others. He was imprisoned, beaten, chased out of town, shipwrecked, stoned and ultimately martyred for his teachings. Yet he remained faithful to the mission and was determined to never give up. Paul understood that his life was too short to waste living in fear and instead remained a bold witness for Christ until his death.

1. Do you agree with Tebow that your responsibility as an athlete is to reach out to your teammates, coaches, competitors, etc., with the message of the Gospel?

2. What are some ways that you may be able to influence others on your team?

3. What are some fears that you have faced when considering whether or not to share the Gospel with your teammates?

4. Read through 2 Corinthians 11:22-30 and circle all of the hardships and obstacles that Paul had to overcome in order to pursue others with the Gospel. How does Paul's story encourage you to overcome those fears? Now read 2 Timothy 1:7 and comment on Paul's mindset.

WRAPUP

In these two stories, you've seen examples of relentless mission in action. When Jesus was sharing His final few moments on Earth with the disciples, He gave them one last set of instructions—a command that we often refer to as "The Great Commission." The message can be summarized with these words from Mark 16:15 -- "Go into all the world and preach the Gospel to the whole creation."

It was Jesus' way of reminding the disciples that He didn't come to save them from sin just for their freedom or restoring them back to a relationship with God. Certainly those were both significant motivations for Christ's sacrifice on the Cross but His primary reason was bigger. Jesus came to an imperfect world, lived the perfect life and shed His precious blood so that those who accepted Him as their Savior would then become His representatives to others as noted in 2 Corinthians 5:19-20. God pursued us with His love and now expects us to pursue others as part of a relentless mission to which we have all been called. That means living as an example to those around us (teammates, family, friends, etc.), serving them in love and taking those opportunities to share the Gospel message of hope through a relationship with Christ.

Spiritual Training Points

• **Be Different:** God calls us to be set apart. He calls us to a life of holiness and righteousness. It's a life that resists the temptation to cave to the world's system and instead seeks to live like Jesus as an example to others. Read Romans 12:2.

1. What do you think it means to "be different" from the world (give some personal examples)?

• **Serve Others:** Step out and show love for others through compassion and serve their needs. People will take notice and open a door to share the Gospel with them. Read 1 Peter 4:10.

2. What are some examples of loving others or serving others' needs?

• **Share The Gospel:** As you stand out and serve others, they'll want to know why. Jesus commands us to share the Gospel with those around us. Read Matthew 28:19-20.

3. What are some ways that you can share the Gospel with with your teammates?

4. What do you think it might look like to "preach the Gospel" within your team?

5. How might understanding and embracing the fact that "He has committed the message of reconciliation to us" and that "we are ambassadors for Christ" change your outlook on personal evangelism?

6. Take some time to share some of your story—things that may hinder your mission, ways you've shared the Gospel and thoughts on how you might better pursue others in the future.

God has a great purpose for your life. He relentlessly pursues you. In response, you pursue Him through a relationship with Christ. As you grow, you pursue abundant life. This leads to a mission to relentlessly pursue others with the Gospel. Only then will we truly be able to live the relentless life. Go out and live relentlessly for Jesus Christ!

ACCOUNTABILITY

FINDING FAITHFUL FRIENDS

"The wounds of a friend are trustworthy, but the kisses of an enemy are excessive." Proverbs 27:6

Former NFL players, Eric Boles and Jon Kitna, have been part of an accountability group for a number of years. They approach accountability with a combination of full transparency and not letting one another off the hook. They regularly talk about tempting situations, personal finances, anger and pride issues—no subject is off limits. Eric states, "It is not a sin management group where we console one another about the sin but don't do anything about it. Our group doesn't allow one another to get comfortable with their sin." Their mindset is: "Totally understandable, but totally unacceptable."

Accountability: Being answerable to God and at least one other person for my behavior.

1. Have you ever had the type of friendships described by Eric and Jon? Describe the "accountability" you have had with specific people from your past.

2. Is there a specific person on your team with whom you have a high degree of accountability? How is the accountability working for you and for them?

Team Builder: Get a copy of the accountability questions from www.characterthatcounts.org Bring the questions to your next team meeting and discuss the impact of answering these questions on a weekly basis with yourself and your team.

Two men were riding a sleigh during a blizzard. They were extremely cold and terrified they would not reach safety. They came upon another traveler who had fallen in the snow. He was close to death. One of the two men on the sleigh pleaded with the other that they stop and help. The other refused. The concerned one decided to stay, even though the delay could mean his death. His companion left the two of them behind. Working feverishly, the one who stayed to help massage the unconscious man's body. After what seemed like hours of labor, the man responded and began to revive. The two men got up and walked in the snow together, the vigorous work of massage having saved them both. As they walked on, they came upon the sleigh and the man who had refused to stay and help. He was frozen to death.

The energy we spend on relationships is never wasted. Each time we stop to help a near frozen friend, we grow in our own development and character. We need each other. Together we survive. Alone, we freeze and die.

Each of us has weak spots, making us susceptible to the temptations of this world. Though some may fall because of one bad decision, most who get into trouble make a series of minor bad decisions—even decisions that go undetected—that slowly wear down their character and faith. God's Word says that we must stand firm in the faith and guard against falling away (Hebrews 5:14).

Unfortunately, some fall because they don't answer to anyone for their behavior. Choose to make yourself accountable to another person.

Many Christians mistakenly believe they can live a life of integrity without help. That attitude, however, makes us more vulnerable to sin. It ignores the biblical commands to help each other (e.g., Galatians 6:2, Eccl. 4:9-12, Proverbs 27:17).

Nebraska volleyball player Jill McWilliams found that during her playing days for the Cornhuskers she relied heavily upon Christian friends, including the FCA women's Bible study and the Sunday night huddle meetings. "It was important to have people surrounding you who you could really talk to. It was very special to develop those types of friendships."

1. Without revealing names, identify the character qualities of your three best friends. Why are they your best friends? How much do these friends really know about you?

2. What role does accountability currently play in your life? Are you satisfied with it?

3. While many people erroneously believe that accountability is bondage, in reality accountability means freedom. Why is this true?

Being accountable to someone means owning up to past hurts and present shortcomings by committing to positive change. It begins with seeing the need to make changes and having the courage to make it happen with a new plan of action. Every person needs protection from self, along with a safety net. Pride is our biggest enemy. We need to reach a point where we can confess our sins and shortcomings to one another.

We're not meant to walk this journey alone. Maintaining integrity requires the encouragement of accountability. People—especially close friends—keep us pumped up. They communicate "you can do it, you can make it" a dozen different ways. At David's low-water mark, Jonathan stepped in. Right when Elijah was ready to punt, along came Elisha. Paul had Timothy, Silas and Barnabas to help him.

Here's what is against us: we are traveling through life unconnected and unexamined. We try really hard to maintain an image that we have got it all together, when in reality we don't. Inside, we are often falling apart and desperately crying for help, but we don't have the courage to talk to someone. This is exactly the reason we need to open up our hearts to others.

Don't fall into the trap of isolation. Isolation is the Christian's silent enemy because it promotes a belief that you can be strong in your own power. Living the Christian life is a "we" thing not a "me" thing. There is an old African proverb that states, "If you want to go fast, go alone. If you want to go far, go together."

Accountability involves a regular check-in time to ask the hard questions and point out blind spots. Accountability also involves helping friends and teammates live up to their commitments. Through involvement in each other's lives you can really help out one another, especially when temptations hit. Teammates, coaches, pastors, counselors and our parents can help us set personal goals and then provide accountability to keep us on track.

1. React to this statement: "To live an unaccountable life is to flirt with danger." Why is this true or false?

2. Have you been corrected or criticized by a coach or a teammate recently? How did you respond? Did you hold yourself accountable or make an excuse?

3. If you needed correction in your relationship with God, who would be the one person you would want to do it? Why?

4. Is there anyone in your life asking you about real issues that you face on a daily basis? If there isn't, would you be interested in establishing an accountability relationship? Why or why not?

Every day is filled with slippery slopes and landmines that have the potential to create long-term destructive consequences and hardship in life. Accountability aids you in being strong in the Lord when facing temptations and challenges. It not only helps in making better decisions and choices, but it also strengthens the resolve of my partner(s) too. Relentlessly pursue accountability by voluntarily being answerable to at least one other person for your character and conduct.

CHEERFUL

"Anxiety in a man's heart weighs it down, but a good word cheers it up." Proverbs 12:25

My daughter's 11-12 year old softball team had to be one of the worst ever. At our first practice, the girls couldn't throw, catch or hit. I whispered to my fellow coaches it would be a miracle if we won even one game. However, we agreed as coaches that our lips would only speak encouraging words; we would commit to cheerfulness at our practices and games. We decided not to worry about our regular season record, but focus on our ultimate goal: the year-end tournament.

At our first game, my worst fears came true. We were slaughtered 19-2 by a very mediocre team. However, we coaches found positive things to say about the girls' performance. Week after week, the losses mounted but our cheerfulness stayed constant.

Cheerful: Expressing encouragement, approval or congratulations at the proper time.

1. Would you describe your past and current coaches as "cheerful?" Why or why not?

2. Who is the most cheerful coach you have ever played for? How did you feel?

Team Builder: On a slip of paper, write one sentence "cheerful notes" to each of your teammates. After everyone is done, give the notes to the people you wrote about. After everyone has read his notes, comment on how these words made you feel.

Of our first 13 games, we somehow managed to win two. In games #14 and #15, the girls' performance improved dramatically, and we won our last two games of the regular season.

With a 4-11 record, we decided to hold our year-end party prior to the tournament, in case we ended up losing quickly. We were seeded #13 of 16 teams. At the party, each girl was publicly affirmed in front of her teammates, family and friends for the contributions she had made during the season. It was an exciting night for each of the girls. On the way home from the party, my daughter Brooke asked me a very interesting question. She said, "Dad, who do you think we'll play in the championship game?" I almost burst out in laughter but maintained my poise and replied, "Well, I think we will play the team who finished with a 23-1 record (including winning two optional tournaments)." Brooke agreed.

Well to make a long story short, my daughter's improbable prediction became a reality as our team marched undefeated through the year end tournament-all the way to the championship. We absolutely shocked our opponents and the entire league. We were beaten in the final game, finishing second place, but I was so proud of our team, our coaches and our parents. Each person had made a commitment to be cheerful, and the results were amazing.

Abraham Lincoln once remarked, "Most folks are about as happy as they make up their minds to be." Anyone who has taken the time to observe the world's happy ones usually finds common traits. People who are cheerful are eager to share their joy with others. If being happy is something we "make up our minds to be," then be enthusiastic to help others be happy first. We actually get more as we give more. In fact, if we don't give we can't keep what we have. Cheerfulness is all about sharing it with others.

Being cheerful can brighten anyone's day. There are physical, psychological and spiritual rewards of cheerfulness because it is contagious. It is one of those rare treasures which is multiplied when given away.

1. How can being cheerful radically change your school, your team, your family and your community?

2. Look at each of these words: encouragement, approval and congratulations. What is the best way to incorporate these words into your life on a daily basis?

3. Is cheerfulness a "natural" or "learned" gift? What role does God play in making you cheerful?

Barnabas was known for his cheerfulness. In fact his name is translated as "son of encourager." He had a way of blessing everyone he interacted with and drawing out the best in them. In the book of Acts, Paul and Barnabas worked together well but one day they had a conflict about taking John Mark with them on a mission trip. Barnabas was willing to reach out to people who were less than perfect. The young John Mark had abandoned his ministry duties on an earlier trip to Cyprus, but Barnabas never gave up on him. Through Barnabas's encouragement, John Mark was given a second chance.

Barnabas had the unique ability to change the atmosphere around him, because he encouraged people. Whenever people were around Barnabas, their spirits were lifted, and their faith was strengthened. Guidance, help and direction is never a solo search. Growth in our lives occurs when we are surrounded and immersed in cheerful relationships. We get better and find our way in groups, not by ourselves. Positive connection with others provides guidance, encouragement and prayer support. There is lots of laughter when we are in the midst of cheerful people. Living life with others is just plain fun.

What produces cheerfulness? Cheerfulness is not the absence of trouble, but the presence of Christ. Our greatest source of cheer is eternal salvation. Because cheerfulness comes from having a genuine relationship with Christ, anything hindering that fellowship will diminish it. Jesus reminds us that cheerfulness comes by keeping the commands of the Lord (read John 15:10-13).

Jesus, remove negative attitudes and replace it with cheerfulness. Amen.

1. Go on a Bible search in the book of Acts looking for the various stories where Barnabas encouraged people. What lessons can you learn from his life? How can you become more like a Barnabas?

2. Most cheerful people are busy enjoying work right up to the time they draw their last breath. A well-known writer said, "If you observe a really happy man, you will find him building a boat, writing a symphony, educating his son, growing roses in his garden, or looking for dinosaur eggs in the Gobi Desert. He will have become aware that he is happy in the course of living life fully." Do you believe this statement is true? Why or why not?

3. Are you considered to be a cheerful person? Why or why not? What could help you become even more cheerful?

4. Who is someone you know who needs cheered up? What specific act could you do to help them?

Proverbs 12:25 says, "Anxiety in a man's heart weighs it down, but a good word cheers it up." A cheerful spirit is contagious. You can brighten anyone's day through a smile, a high five, a pat on the back, the gift of your time, a joyous attitude, laughter or an encouraging word. Make a decision to do everything in your power to live cheerfully by looking for the good in all things, not giving into discouragement, not allowing your emotions to rule your mind and taking time out to laugh and sing every day.

COMPASSION

GIVING THROUGH YOUR ACTIONS

"and whoever wants to be first among you must be a slave to all. For even the Son of Man did not come to be served, but to serve, and to give His life—a ransom for many." Mark 10:44-45

Our nation has experienced numerous tragedies in the recent past, including Hurricane Katrina. Ex-NFL quarterback Danny Wuerffel has devoted his life to serving the people of New Orleans' through Desire Street Ministries. Danny's home and ministry location were destroyed in Katrina. "I have wept over our city, thinking about the many families and children who drowned in their homes," he said. "It's an incredibly sad thing. At the same time, we've experienced times of incredible joy and vision and see an opportunity to do greater good than we've ever done before. We're very resolved and very determined and passionate about helping people."

Compassion: Investing whatever is necessary to heal the hurts of others by the willingness to bear their pain.

1. What remembrances do you have of September 11, 2001, Hurricane Katrina or other national tragedies?

2. What acts of compassion did you hear of or participate in during these tragic events?

Team Builder: Present Red Bandannas and invite your team to join the "Fellowship of the Red Bandanna." See the website: www.redbandanna.org for details. Then, as a group determine what you can do to put your compassion into action.

As stories began to emerge from survivors of the South Tower of the World Trade Center, several mentioned a mysterious young man who stepped out of the smoke and horror to lead them to safety. They did not know this man who saved their lives, but this they did remember: Wrapped around his mouth and nose was a red bandanna.

For 76 minutes, the man in the red bandanna barked orders leading people to safety down stairwells. He said, "I found the stairs, follow me." He carried one woman down fifteen flights on his back, while leading others to safety, urged them to keep going down, then headed back up. Upstairs, a badly injured woman was sitting on a radiator when the man wearing the red bandanna came running and said, "Follow me. I know the way out. I will lead you to safety." Then he led several survivors to a stairwell that took them to safety. He was never seen alive again. Six months later, on March 19, 2002, the body of the man with the red bandanna was found intact alongside firefighters in a makeshift command center in the South Tower lobby, buried under 110 stories of rubble.

Slowly the story began to come out. Welles Crowther graduated from Boston College where he played lacrosse, always carrying his trademark red bandanna. In high school Welles was the kid who would feed the puck to the hockey team's lowest-scoring player, hoping to give his teammate his first goal. At 16 he became a junior volunteer firefighter, following in his dad's footsteps. After college he joined Sandler O'Neil and Partners, working on the 104th floor of the South Tower. He always carried change to give to street people. His dream was to become a firefighter or public servant. On September 11, 2001, at the age of 24, Welles Crowther became both, and also a hero—the "man in the red bandanna."

Our world is in desperate need of people willing to go up while everyone else is coming down—to rescue lost men and women leading them to the safety of the cross of Christ. The Fellowship of the Red Bandanna is offered to those who are willing to train, serve, and make a sacrifice to help hurting others.

1. Discuss the compassion of Welles Crowther and how it compares to what you would have done if you faced similar circumstances (in your response think about Welles' compassion both before 9/11 and on 9/11).

2. What is your reaction to Danny Wuerffel's compassion?

3. Would you describe yourself as compassionate? Why or why not?

WRAPUP

Living for Christ means taking a stand to show compassion and taking active steps to draw others to God. Showing compassion is impossible without responding to needs in tangible, measurable ways.

Three men saw a wounded traveler by the side of the road. The first one must have felt sympathy (feeling sorry for people who are hurting) as he passed by. The second indicated empathy (feeling the pain with hurting people) as he came over and looked at him, but the third had compassion (doing something about the pain) as he stopped and helped him. The third man was the Good Samaritan as described in Luke 10:30-37.

Thomas Jefferson once stated, "When the heart is right the feet are swift." Real compassion begins with acts, rather than ideas. Compassion is realized by acting out Biblically—regardless of how we feel or think.

God loves a cheerful, compassionate giver who responds to the needs of others (2 Corinthians 9:7). Compassionate people have swift feet and terrific energy! When the Israelites gave themselves and their belongings to construct the tabernacle in the wilderness, their energy was so evident they had to be told not to give anymore (Exodus 36:6-7).

When the people in Jerusalem rallied around Nehemiah and rebuilt the wall, their swiftness resulted in record-breaking achievement (Nehemiah 2:17-18, 4:6, 6:15-16). In everything you do, show your compassion to those needing help by remembering Jesus' words: "It is more blessed to give than to receive."

Have you ever noticed how contagious a compassionate, generous spirit becomes? Not only do we feel great, others do as well. There is unmatched joy in learning that something you've said or done has been meaningful to another, especially when you do it without any thought of receiving anything in return. Helping others in any way—with a tangible act of kindness, a smile, a nod or a pat on the back— makes people feel better.

1. Review the Good Samaritan and Nehemiah story and make observations from these passages.

2. React and respond to the following statement: "Real compassion begins with acts, rather than ideas. Wisdom teaches us that you can act your way into a new way of thinking better than think your way into a new way of acting. We should do the right thing first, regardless of our feelings and allow our feelings to catch up later. Spiritual growth and development is realized by acting out Biblical precepts and principles—regardless of how we feel or think about them. If we embrace opportunities without hesitation, they will change us."

3. Think of a friend who needs your compassion right now. What could you do to help them?

Welles Crowther, the Good Samaritan and Nehemiah were all relentless with their compassion. They chose to serve others when it would have been much easier for them to care only about themselves. Look for opportunities to give to others, including those on your team, serving them above your own needs and desires (Philippians 2:3). Responding to a need and doing whatever is necessary to meet those needs brings comfort to others.

DETERMINATION

NEVER GIVE UP

"We are pressured in every way but not crushed; we are perplexed but not in despair; we are persecuted but not abandoned; we are struck down but not destroyed." 2 Cor. 4:8-9

Noelle Pikus-Pace began her skeleton racing career in 2001 and she won her first overall World Cup title in 2004 becoming the first American to win that award. As the defending world champion she was a favorite to win the gold medal in the 2006 Olympic Games. But her medal ambitions were seriously jeopardized in October 2005 when her right leg was broken from a runaway bobsled. Pikus-Pace made a miraculous recovery, but her attempt to make the 2006 U.S. Olympic Team fell short. Noelle did her part. Her will, determination and hard work placed her in the right spot at the right time for a spot on the podium. But her sport, the system and a goofy federation governing the event played roles in preventing her from competing. Her story was told in the critically acclaimed documentary "114 Days: The Race To Save A Dream." One person who saw the documentary stated, "I felt betrayed for Noelle. I wanted to find someone and knock the snot out of them. The system failed her."

Determination: Working intently to accomplish goals regardless of the opposition.

1. What can you learn from Noelle's story?

2. Share a time when you have seen determination in action.

Team Builder: As a team, view and discuss the "114 Days, the Race to Save a Dream" by Matt Fults.

You don't have to know the sport of skeleton to get the point of this story. The human drama, a dream to succeed, a push by a world-class athlete to go beyond what a normal human should have to endure-only to have a game of numbers and points end her quest.

The story is a challenge to either give up or get up. Pikus-Pace chose to get up after being hit by a runaway bobsled, steered by an inexperienced crew scared spitless. The bobsled hurtled down the track at 60 miles an hour, overshot the stop area on October 19, 2005 and plowed into Noelle, breaking her right leg.

Determined to compete in the Olympics slated to begin 114 days from the accident, Noelle had a titanium rod surgically inserted in her leg. In two weeks, she was walking. By the first week of December, she was competing in Austria, a miracle comeback. In January, she finished fifth in a race in Germany, placing ahead of every other American competitor, none of whom even made the top 10. She did this using a new sled, and she hadn't even gotten her timing down.

However, Noelle was declared unqualified to compete in the Olympics because she hadn't accumulated enough points through a season of competition scattered across the globe. Even a plea for an exemption to the International Olympic Committee citing her injury, her recovery, her increased performance capability in the span of time most people with her injury would have needed half a year just to walk, was to no avail. She was out.

Remarkably, Pikus-Pace did not let the 2006 events deter her dream. After taking time away from the sport for several years to give birth to a daughter in 2008, she returned to competition and finished in fourth place at the 2010 Olympic Games in Vancouver, Canada. After retiring again for a couple of seasons, she returned to competition in 2012, and won her first World Cup race in January 2013 in Germany, her first since 2004.

Almost every day we encounter people like Pikus-Pace who are seriously thinking about embarking on a daring and possibly frightening journey. It may be a coach, teammate, friend or even brother, sister, or parent. Urge them on by affirming them. Let them know you are behind them and then fervently pray for them. Too many stop because so few say, "Go!!"

1. When the smiling, bubbly Pikus-Pace finally realized she wouldn't make the 2006 Olympic team, in spite of the miracles, she broke down in tears. How do you respond when your determined efforts are shattered? Where do you go to find hope?

2. Describe a time when you, a teammate or a team showed great determination. What ultimately happened?

3. What are the keys to determination?

WRAPUP

After one to four years at sea, the king salmon determines to head home—back to the stream where it hatched. Swimming against the fierce river currents and leaping up waterfalls, the mighty salmon increases its daily speed as it covers the hundreds of miles home. Determination gives us resolve to keep going in spite of roadblocks. No matter how daunting the task, to be determined is to see it through despite the obstacles facing us.

God's Word stresses the importance of personal determination. The Lord assures us His glory is the goal (1 Corinthians 10:31), not man's approval. Furthermore, when He tells us to love, He tells us to do it fervently (1 Peter 4:8). When maintaining a friendship, it is to be devoted (Romans 12:10). When steering clear of evil, we are told to stay away from even the appearance of it (1 Thessalonians 5:22). When seeing a brother or sister in need, we are to bear the burden sacrificially (Galatians 6:1-2), not stay at a safe distance. When it comes to my sport, I am to be disciplined (2 Thessalonians 3:7-8) and diligent (1 Thessalonians 2:9). The Scriptures abound with exhortations to go above and beyond the required call of duty- to a dedication which persists against opposition, doing my tasks with excellence.

Paul's words in Philippians 3:12-14 say press on for the goal and the prize found in Christ Jesus. God calls us to never go backward. Attempt something great for God, and do it with all your might. Few things are more rewarding than the exhilaration of achievement after wholehearted effort. The stronger the current opposing us, the sweeter the victory will be.

Christians need to persist against opposition. We are never finished until the race is done. Our adversary, the devil, tries to discourage us constantly, but through determination, we can accomplish our goals in spite of opposition.

1. Review the Bible passages noted above and discuss the impact of each scripture with your current team.

2. How much do you listen to "naysayers" and those who talk negative? How can you best respond with an attitude of determination?

3. Have you ever felt like quitting something but then did not? How did it make you feel to not quit? How does quitting impact other people?

4. How important is affirmation and encouraging words in the midst of difficult situations? Are you an encourager? Share a time when you encouraged someone going through a tough experience or when you were lifted up by another person.

RELENTLESS

The Apostle Paul was relentless when he wrote these words in 2 Corinthians 4:8-9, "We are pressured in every way but not crushed; we are perplexed but not in despair; we are persecuted but not abandoned; we are struck down but not destroyed." Obstacles don't have to stop you. If you run into a wall, don't turn around or give up. Pray and ask God how to climb over it, go through it or work your way around it.

ENTHUSIASM

PUSHING TO NEW LEVELS

"Sing to Yahweh, for He has done glorious things. Let this be known throughout the earth. Cry out and sing, citizen of Zion, for the Holy One of Israel is among you in His greatness." Isaiah 12:5-6

James McElwain had done everything with enthusiasm for the Greece Athena (N.Y.) High School basketball team-kept stats, ran the clock and handed out water bottles. At 5-feet-6 and considered too short to play, he opted to be the manager. McElwain, who is autistic and usually sat on the end of the bench in a white shirt and black tie, was given a new role for the last home game of his senior year when he suited up for the first time.

With his team way ahead, McElwain was put into the game with four minutes remaining. He poured in 20 points, including 6 of 10 three point shots, as the crowd went wild. "As soon as the first shot went in, that's when I started to get going," James said. "I ended my career on the right note. I was hotter than a pistol." He was carried off the court on his teammates' shoulders.

Enthusiasm: Expressing lively, absorbing interest in each task as I give it my best effort.

1. What role does enthusiasm play on your team(s)?

2. Who is the most enthusiastic person on your team? Describe his or her impact.

Team Builder: The amazing story of James McElwain has been heavily documented. Do a google search on James and download the video footage of what happened in his final ball game. Watch and discuss it with your team.

The inspiring story of James McElwain enthuses me. Watching the video footage of his shots, tears welled up in my eyes as I observed the response of his teammates and the crowd literally going crazy.

Enthusiasm goes a long way. Enthusiastic teams have a far better chance of achieving success than those who lack spirit and desire. A negative attitude results in defeat while those who encourage their teammates will actually inspire others toward a higher performance.

One team I admired for years was the Pacific Lutheran University football team, out of Tacoma, Washington. Their head coach, Frosty Westering, brimmed with enthusiasm. He was able to take ordinary players and turn them into superstars. His enthusiastic approach to life transformed these young players. Frosty's approach was unconventional as he spent little time on the Xs and Os. One of his favorite football activities was taking his team to the beach and having them play a variety of relay games. His mastery as a coach was his ability to enthuse his players. Westering compiled an incredible 305-96-7 overall record (.756 winning percentage) in 40 seasons as a college coach, including four national championships. Westering's players over four decades experienced the "Frosty Philosophy": That you could team-build without tearing anyone down. That you could get athletes to play their hearts out for each other without screaming at them. He believed winning was "a by-product of learning to live decently," as he told *Sports Illustrated* in a 1994 story that highlighted his unorthodox methods.

"He had the heart to do things a different way to influence kids," said Stacey, who like her siblings and mom did everything from helping with team laundry to chalking the lines on the field. One of her brothers, Scott Westering, is currently Pacific Lutheran's head football coach. "My dad could have moved to a bigger program," Stacey said. "But to stay at that level gave him the freedom to coach the way he believed helped players become better people. He had a whole philosophy on the 'inner game,' and what it took for players to believe in themselves and each other."

1. Share a time when your enthusiasm inspired others. Describe what happened and the impact of your actions upon the other players.

2. Discuss each of these five statements and how each could impact your team:
   - I will put my whole heart into what I do.
   - I will treat every role on the team as important.
   - I will be an energy-giver, not an energy-drainer.
   - I will smile and seek creative ways to encourage my team.
   - I will let Jesus Christ shine through my life.

WRAPUP

If you are not enthusiastic in our efforts toward God as we should be, it's important to ask why. The following four reasons explain why most people are so complacent. We don't take God more seriously because:

1. We don't think we need to. We incorrectly believe our salvation is assured no matter what we do.

2. We don't think we have to. Some are interested only in the bare minimums.

3. We're fearful and discouraged. Dragged down by past struggles, we're doubtful it will do any good to try again so pessimism takes over.

4, We're lazy. Like the lukewarm Laodiceans (Revelation 3:15-18), we're negligent procrastinators.

To be enthusiastic is to be energized and inspired by God, giving each task our best effort. A Biblical counterpart to this word is fervent. To be fervent in spirit is to boil with heat; to be hot, as in boiling with genuine love for God and others. Another Biblical term for enthusiasm is zeal meaning excitement of mind, ardor, or fervor of spirit in pursuing or defending someone or something. Every Christian is at his best when he adds enthusiasm to his situations.

Our enthusiasm for God should exceed our sport. Praising God should be a powerful time! He wants us to glorify Him and "make a joyful noise." Isaiah 12:5-6 states when the time comes to be with God, be enthusiastic!

We live in a world of apathy. So many people are simply existing rather than truly living. Enthusiasm deters apathy. Just knowing Christ personally should change everything about how we live. In Revelation 3:20 we are reminded of the adventure God is calling us to, "Here I am! I stand at the door and knock. If anyone hears my voice and opens the door, I will come in and eat with him, and he with me." My relationship with God, through His Son Jesus Christ, gets me out of bed in the morning. I can't wait to see what He will accomplish each and every day of my life. How about you? Are you approaching life every day with enthusiasm?

Enthusiastically embrace this fresh beginning called "today." God specializes in taking common, simple items and working them into miracles. You and I are the results of transformation.

1. It has been said, "No one keeps up his enthusiasm automatically. Enthusiasm must be nourished with new actions, new aspirations, new efforts, new visions." Do you believe this is true? Why? How does God fit into this quote?

2. David's enthusiastic response when the Ark of the Covenant was returned to its proper place in 2 Samuel 6 (specifically verses 14 & 15). Read this story and comment whether David acted appropriately. How do you respond when you are excited about something?

Enthusiastically embrace the fresh beginning of each new day. God specializes in taking common, simple items (bread, fish, a manger, a cross and even ordinary people) and working miracles. As one of those miracles, an enthusiastic attitude is one of the greatest ways you can show others the Christ who is actively working in your life. When you are enthused, you are proclaiming the truth of Psalm 150:6, "Let everything that breathes praise the Lord. Hallelujah!" Your relentless enthusiasm will give you an opportunity to share your joy with others and exalt Christ.

FAITH

GETTING INTO THE WHEELBARROW

"Now without faith it is impossible to please God, for the one who draws near to Him must believe that He exists and rewards those who seek Him."
Hebrews 11:6

There is a story of a tightrope walker who tied his rope across a waterfall, then asked the crowd that gathered if they believed he could walk across. "Yes!" they yelled, and he did. He then asked how many believed he could walk across the falls on the rope pushing a wheelbarrow. "Yes, you can do it!" they screamed, and he did. He then asked how many believed he could do the same thing, but this time with a person in the wheelbarrow. "Oh yes! We believe it!" they exclaimed. He asked, "Which one of you will be that person?" No one responded.

Faith: Developing an unshakable confidence in God and acting upon it.

1. Describe a time when you had to place your faith in someone other than yourself. What did you learn?

2. What role does your faith play in your sports career? How do you feel when other people talk about their faith in television or radio interviews?

Team Builder: Blindfold two volunteers and move far away. Tell the rest of the group to begin shouting as loudly as they can, all at the same time, instructing how the volunteers can reach you. Next, remove the blindfold from one person. Have him come alongside the remaining blindfolded person, not touching but quietly instructing him. Discuss how this experience relates to our faith in God.

Faith is more than saying: "I believe." To believe in what you can see requires no faith. However, believing in something you cannot see, and placing confidence in its reality as if you could see, hear, taste, touch, and smell, is genuine faith. It is having confidence to get into the wheelbarrow and trust the one pushing. Faith is to be willing to act upon belief.

As a young boy, my brothers and I loved jumping off our triple decker bunk bed into the arms of our dad. We would beg him to come outside so we could jump out of the trees into his arms. At the pool, we spent hours launching ourselves off the edge, once again into his arms. Our dad proved himself faithful by always catching us. Faith in God is trusting He will do the same.

One great story of faith centers on Abraham. God told Abraham He would make him and his descendants a great nation (Genesis 12:2,7). But there was a huge problem with God's promise because Abraham and Sarah had no children and were way past child bearing years. Abraham believed God and waited patiently on Him to fulfill His promise. Isaac was born when he was 100 years old and Sarah was 90.

A few years later, Abraham's faith was further tested. Hebrews 11:17-19 tells us that by faith Abraham offered Isaac as a sacrifice. Abraham believed God could raise the dead, and figuratively speaking, he received Isaac back from death. The faith of Abraham is testimony that he believed and trusted God. As Hebrews 11:1 and 6 states, "Now faith is being sure of what we hope for and certain of what we do not see...and without faith it is impossible to please God, because anyone who comes to him must believe that he exists and that he rewards those who earnestly seek him." Just as Abraham had faith, God wants us to.

Faith is one part of the great triad: faith, hope and love. All three of these spiritual attributes look to the future through the eyes of trust. Working together, they produce the "work of faith," the "labor of love," and the "patience of hope" (1 Thessalonians 1:3). By faith, we seek to please God because we love Him.

1. Name someone you know that has an active, faith filled life with Jesus Christ. What type of influence does his/her life have upon your own?

2. What role does trust play in having faith?

3. How is faith in God lived out in your life?

4. What do you think of when you hear the term "taking a leap of faith?" Is this proper or not?

Hebrews 11 is often called the "Hall of Faith." It has numerous examples of men and women who took God at His word and trusted Him with the results. One example of this is Enoch, described in Genesis 5:24 as a man "who walked with God." His walk, based on faith, had remarkable results, as noted in Hebrews 11:5. Enoch pleased God, the text says, by faith. Does this mean just "intellectual faith" pleases God? No, we must have faith that diligently reaches toward God in a trust that is both hopeful and loving. "For we walk by faith, not by sight....we make it our aim, whether present or absent, to be well pleasing to Him" (2 Corinthians 5:7-9). We need to understand that "pleasing God" is realized by obedience.

The foundation of our existence is trusting God, who makes life worth living. Faith is trusting in God's providence and care. Faith is an attitude which declares, "I don't know what God is doing, but I believe that whatever it is, it's His best for my life." A person who believes does not need all the answers because he has the presence and love of Christ. God's intimate presence comforts and gives us assurance in the midst of challenges. We are like infants being held in the strong, safe arms of our parent.

Faith enables us to give up what seems good on the surface and patiently wait for what we know is best—after all, "Good things come to those who wait." Although sometimes tempted to say "yes" to something that may not be God's best, we need to faithfully choose to say "no" to anything that will compromise our relationship with God.

A high school basketball coach was asked how he managed to maintain his faith in the midst of a turbulent and chaotic season. He said, "I have a very important partnership with God. I agreed to place my complete trust in God, and He agreed to do the worrying. I haven't had a worry since. He's kept his bargain, and so have I." This coach is living out his faith every single day.

Have you put your full faith and trust in God, giving every area of your life to Him? Or do you just say you trust Him, refusing to get in the wheelbarrow and let Him guide you? The answers to these questions will impact your eternal home.

1. How well do you respond when life situations don't go like you've planned? What role does faith play in the midst of these challenges?

2. How would you describe your own faith in Jesus Christ? Are you certain that if you were to die tonight that you would spend eternity in heaven? Why are you sure or not sure?

Hebrews 11:6 reminds us that without faith it is impossible to please God. We must draw near to Him and truly believe in Him with a relentless faith. God promises us that those who do this will receive a great reward in heaven someday. Relentless faith has the mindset of "I do not know what the future holds, but I know who holds the future." Do you have faith in yourself or faith in God? Faith in self will ultimately be futile. If your faith is in God, you will not be disappointed—now and for all eternity.

FORGIVENESS

HAPPINESS = FORGIVING EASILY

"And whenever you stand praying, if you have anything against anyone, forgive him, so that your Father in heaven will also forgive you your wrongdoing." Mark 11:25

Chris Webber calls for the "timeout" and he along with his Fab Five teammates lose their opportunity to win the '93 championship game. With no timeouts left, he received a technical that cost them the game.

In every ball game mistakes are made—errant throws, dropped balls, strikeouts or falling down at inopportune moments. Few mistakes are as costly as Chris Webber's, but many professionals blow it during televised games for the whole world to see. Are these athletes not allowed to play anymore? Not at all. In fact, the player who made the mistake is often relied on immediately by his teammates to do it right on the next possession.

Forgiveness: Clearing the record of those who have wronged me and not holding their past offenses against them.

1. Have you ever blown it in a game? How did your teammates react? The fans? How did their reactions make you feel?

2. What advice would you give a teammate if he/she made a critical mistake at the end of a game costing your team a win?

Team Builder: Ask each person to find a partner and share his most humiliating moment in sports (dropping a pass, shooting a game-losing airball, etc.). What bearing did it have upon the game? Have a few people share their stories with the entire group.

All of us have been hurt by someone who we deeply care about. These hurts can leave us angry and bitter. God's solution? "Get rid of all bitterness, rage and anger, brawling and slander, along with every form of malice. Be kind and compassionate to one another, forgiving each other, just as in Christ God forgave you" (Ephesians 4:31-32). If we are going to experience God fully, we must choose to forgive.

A number of studies reveal it is not great wealth that makes people happy, but having friends and forgiveness. Commenting on these findings in a *USA Today* article, Marilyn Elias says, "The happiest people surround themselves with family and friends, don't care about keeping up with the Joneses next door, lose themselves in daily activities, and most important, forgive easily."

An unforgiving spirit is often the last emotional fortress we yield to God. Even as Christians, we often cling to anger and bitterness, feeling that those who have wronged us should suffer for their offenses. However, when we realize how much God has forgiven us, we must compel ourselves to extend mercy

(Colossians 3:12-13). Forgiving others is God's command to us and promises a life full of love, peace, thankfulness, and joy. Freely we have been forgiven; let us freely forgive.

One person said, "Forgiveness is agreeing to live with the consequences of another person's sin. Forgiveness is costly; we pay the price of the evil we forgive. Yet you're going to live with those consequences whether you want to or not; your only choice is whether you will do so in the bondage of bitterness or the freedom of forgiveness. That's how Jesus forgave you—He took the consequences of your sin upon Himself. All true forgiveness is substitutional, because no one really forgives without bearing the penalty of the other person's sin."

The forgiveness God gives is genuinely "Good News." We have all made mistakes we regret, but many of us have seen blame and denial modeled as responses to sin, and these only produce more sinful behavior. God is the God of second chances....and third chances....and fourth chances....and on and on (see Psalm 86:5). The forgiveness of God washes us clean.

1. Think of a situation outside of sports when you've made an obvious mistake. How did you feel? How did others around you react? How do you think Jesus reacted?

2. Respond to this quote: "When it seems you can't forgive, remember how much you've been forgiven." Discuss the forgiveness you have been extended by Jesus Christ. How does this impact you?

3. Do you forgive others easily? Why or why not?

Why then do we forgive? Because Christ forgave us. God the Father "made Him who knew no sin to be sin on our behalf, that we might become the righteousness of God in Him" (2 Corinthians 5:21). Where is the justice? The cross makes forgiveness legally and morally right: "For the death that He died, He died to sin, once for all" (Romans 6:10).

So how do you forgive from the heart? First you must acknowledge the hurt and hate—the emotional core of your soul. Simply brushing aside the pain is something that many Christians mistakenly believe they should do because they are Christians, but that's a cover-up. We need to let God bring the pain to the surface so He can deal with it. Then healing can begin.

Ask God to bring to your mind those you need to forgive. Make a list of all who have offended you. Since God has forgiven them by His grace, you can forgive them too. For each person on your list, say: "Lord, I forgive (name) for (offenses)." Keep praying about each individual until you are sure that all the remembered pain has been dealt with. Don't try to rationalize or explain the offender's behavior. Forgiveness deals with your pain, not another's behavior. Remember: Positive feelings will follow in time; freeing yourself from the pain of the past is the critical issue.

Forgiving is tough. Letting go of past wrongs, deep resentments, or personal betrayals can seem impossible. However, counselors, psychologists and even medical doctors have seen miracles occur because of the healing power of forgiveness. It is often a crucial component to emotional recovery, family reconciliations, and in some cases, improved physical health.

1. Peter blew it when he denied Jesus three times just prior to His crucifixion. Read the entire story in Luke 22:54-62 and Matthew 26:57-75 and answer the following questions:

a. Why did Peter deny Jesus three times?

b. What impact did this have on Peter and on Jesus?

c. What ultimately resulted following this major mistake?

2. Share a time when you were extended forgiveness and how it felt to be forgiven.

3. Is there a current situation on your team or at school where forgiveness is needed? If so, make plans right now to get this situation resolved by asking your team to help you follow through with your commitment to forgive.

4. Is there anyone you need to personally forgive? I encourage you to take the first step towards reconciliation.

RELENTLESS

We serve an amazing God who has freely extended His forgiveness to us through the shed blood of Jesus Christ. With your debt fully forgiven by Christ, you are now challenged to forgive others as well. When you choose to forgive, you release them by turning the person and the situation over to God. It is releasing the anger and the responsibility for judging them to the Lord. Just as you ask Jesus to "forgive us our debts" each day, you must ask Him to help you "forgive our debtors."

OBEDIENCE

"There is a way that seems right to a man, but its end is the way to death."
Proverbs 14:12

Kodie McWilliams is one of my heroes. For the past several years, she has represented the state of Missouri at the Aquatics competition at the Special Olympics National Games. She was born with Down Syndrome, yet her dreams to win Olympic gold have been realized multiple times. Her pool workouts, combined with her time in the gym with weights, situps, pushups and treadmill work makes her a force in the competition. She has mastered the flip turn and people are amazed with her double kick butterfly.

Have you ever been part of a Special Olympics event? The sacrifice and obedience of the volunteers and participants is remarkable. From the volunteers, there are sacrifices of time and energy to make sure each

participant is valued. With the participants, you see an amazing degree of obedience as each competitor attempts to follow the rules precisely even though he may not be able to fully comprehend them. The key for these Olympians is to compete fairly and to the best of their abilities. One parent said, "Everyone walks away as a winner at these events."

Obedience: Fulfilling instructions so that the one I am serving will be fully satisfied and pleased.

1. Have you ever participated in a Special Olympics event? If so, share your experience with the entire group.

Team Builder: Have your team volunteer to be part of a Special Olympics event. Make observations about what you learned from the day and share those at your next team meeting.

A key strategic move in baseball is when the manager asks a player to lay down a sacrifice bunt or hit a ball to the right side of the infield. This play allows a runner to advance a base while the hitter is retired. The batter's personal goals, including the desire to improve his own statistics, are not as important as obedience to the manager's directive. Players who do not follow the instructions to sacrifice will find themselves sitting on the bench.

We are told in James 2:23 that "Abraham believed God." Therefore, he obeyed when God said, "Get out of your country" (Genesis 12:1). The habit of obedience is revealed numerous times each day. Obedience indicates you are headed in the right direction toward deeper intimacy with God by trusting him completely.

As a Christian, to sacrifice is a willingness to say no to anything which comes in the way of our relationship with God. No sacrifice is too great when it comes to obeying. Why did Jesus Christ come to earth? He came to be obedient to His Father. Jesus Christ was the ultimate sacrifice.

Even though He was completely innocent, He offered Himself as a sacrifice for others, including His enemies. He became our substitute, placing our sin directly on Himself, taking it to the cross. It was a sacrificial act of obedience by Jesus Christ, the Son of God (Philippians 2:5-11).

While Jesus was completely obedient, King Saul revealed his disobedience. The Lord's instructions to Saul in 1 Samuel 15 were very specific. He was to totally destroy the Amalekites. Nothing, including livestock, was to be spared. Saul killed their army, but he spared King Agag. He also kept the finest livestock, rationalizing his disobedience by sacrificing them to the Lord. When Samuel heard what Saul had done, he was both angry and heartbroken. "Why did you not obey the Lord?" he questioned Saul. "I thought God would be pleased with my sacrifices," Saul whispered. "God wants your obedience rather than your sacrifices," Samuel answered angrily. Saul pleaded for forgiveness but this act of disobedience was the last straw—God rejected him as king over Israel.

1. Comment on the following quote: "Our attitude and actions each play a part in obedience." Why is this true?

2. Is your team obedient to the direction of your coach? Why or why not? What are the consequences of disobedience?

3. Discuss the ramifications of living obediently in the context of your coach, your teammates, at home and with God.

WRAPUP

Saul's story is a dramatic and tragic account of the consequences of disobedience. His life was a series of compromises. While it may seem these are "little compromises" God takes disobedience very seriously. I call it being "One Degree Off." While one degree may seem miniscule initially, as the lines are extended, the gap becomes wider.

- At 90 feet you are off 18 inches
- At 1 mile you are off by 86 feet
- At 60 miles you are off by 1 mile
- At 600 miles you are off by 10 miles
- At 6,000 miles you are off by 100 miles

One person described it this way, "If you were to fly a plane from New York City to Sydney, Australia and you were one degree off, you would land hundreds of miles away from your target destination, somewhere in the Outback." This is what happens when we live "One Degree Off." We will stray from God's path.

In what ways are you compromising and being disobedient? In Saul's case, he thought partial obedience would satisfy God, but from this story we learn that full obedience is the only way to please Him. Today, we find it easy to give up sins which make us feel depressed and weak but how do you handle sinful areas which you find fun, entertaining and pleasurable? For example, we know we shouldn't date an unbeliever, but he or she is just so good looking. We know we shouldn't gossip with our friends, but it's so fun when you have juicy news to spread. God never said we could just keep the "fun sins." He requires us to rid ourselves of every sin without compromise.

Saul deceived himself that he was pleasing God while being disobedient. It's easy for us to do the same. God, through his Word and the conviction of the Holy Spirit must be the final authority over what is right and wrong in our lives. There are times when God may use a coach or a teammate to challenge us in an area that needs to be addressed. It's never fun or easy to be made aware of sin, but it is necessary if you want to avoid sin's

consequences—which are even more painful. Search your heart carefully and ask God to help you be obedient in all areas of your life.

1. How do you feel about the "One Degree Off" illustration? Why is being off one degree a big deal? What are the steps needed to get back in alignment when you get off track?

2. Read 1 Samuel 15:1-26 to get the full story of Saul and his disobedience. Unpack the story and discuss why this was a great disappointment to God.

3. John 14:15 says, "If you love Me, you will keep My commandments." In what ways are you compromising and being disobedient to God and His Word? What do you need to do to change?

FINISH

Little compromises, even just being one degree off, can lead a person to death (Proverbs 14:12). In contrast, Jesus said, "If you love me, you will obey what I command" (John 14:15). Total obedience is the indication of our love for God. When we are connected to Christ we will live a life characterized by obedience to God's precepts and principles. Obedience to God's standards fulfills His promises to us.

PASSIONATE

LAYING IT ALL OUT FOR HIM

"Flee from youthful passions, and pursue righteousness, faith, love, and peace, along with those who call on the Lord from a pure heart."
2 Timothy 2:22

On June 19, 1986, Maryland basketball star Len Bias died of cocaine intoxication two days after being selected by the Boston Celtics as the second overall pick in the NBA draft. His mother, Lonise Bias, had no idea he was using the drug. Since his death, Lonise has been on a passionate crusade conducting workshops and seminars around the country in an effort to stop drug abuse among our nation's youth. She launched the campaign over 25 years ago to cope with her loss and to help parents avoid a similar tragedy. "I have seen a lot of good come out of his death. I believe Len's death helped turn the situation around involving drugs.

Len lost his life to help save others."

Passionate: Having an intense, powerful or compelling emotion and feelings towards others or something.

1. Lonise Bias has been passionate about sharing her son's tragic story with anyone and everyone. Why is she so passionate about sharing the story?

2. Lonise Bias also said, "If Len would have lived he would have entertained you. But in death, he brought life." How can this be true?

Team Builder: Mel Gibson's movie, "The Passion of the Christ" is a powerful picture of the passion of Jesus as He died on the cross. As a team, watch this movie and discuss the passion of Jesus Christ.

I love to be around people who are passionate about life and athletics. People with passion have energy and an attitude which brings out the best in others. Andy Andrews said, "Passion is a product of the heart. Passion is what helps you when you have a dream. Passion breeds conviction and turns mediocrity into excellence! Your passion will motivate others to join you in pursuit of your dream. With passion, you will overcome insurmountable obstacles. You will become unstoppable!"

Throughout my lifetime, I have had the privilege of being around people of passion, and I have always benefited greatly from them. While I have never met Lonise Bias, I know I would like her because she is passionate about helping people.

To see passion personified, we need only to look at Jesus Christ. The word "passion" comes from a Latin word meaning "suffering." The suffering He endured could not have been any more horrific. Even before the Roman guards captured Him in the Garden of Gethsemane, He was sweating drops of blood (Luke 22:44). He literally took the sins of the entire world, past, present and future, upon Himself by experiencing the worst death possible—crucifixion. Only the worst criminals were crucified. Yet it was even more dreadful for Jesus, because He was nailed to the cross by His hands and feet, rather than tied to the cross. Each nail was 6 to 8 inches long and were driven into His wrists and His bound feet. There's a tendon in the wrist that extends to the shoulder. The Roman guards knew when the nails were being hammered into the wrist, the tendon would tear and break, forcing Jesus to use His back muscles to support himself, so He could breathe. For hours on the cross, Jesus endured incredible pain and suffering with each breath.

The beatings, the taunts from the crowd, the gruesome walk on the Viva Delarosa to Calvary and the nails driven into His hands and feet, were all part of God's supreme plan to save mankind. His passion for you and me was what gave Him the will to go the cross for our sins.

One of the most stunning statements Jesus ever made was about His own death and resurrection is found in John 10:17-18. Jesus chose to die. He embraced it because of His complete obedience to His Father (read Philippians 2:5-11).

1. Besides Jesus, who is the most passionate person you know? What do you think fuels their passion?

2. What are you passionate about?

3. Read John 10:7-18. How does the passion of Jesus impact you?

4. Why did Jesus have to die on the cross?

WRAPUP

John Piper said, "Because of this unparalleled passion, God raised Jesus from the dead. It happened three days later. Early Sunday morning he rose from the dead. He appeared numerous times to His disciples for forty days before His ascension to heaven (Acts 1:3). Jesus finished the work God gave him to do, and the resurrection was the proof that God was satisfied." His resurrection proved we were now free from the bondage of death. We are now fully reconciled to God.

The passion of Jesus Christ is the most important event in history and to this day it is still the most explosive topic on planet earth. His death and resurrection is the centerpiece of God's entire plan. The apostle Paul recognized the importance of these events when he penned his words as noted 1 Corinthians 15:13-17, "But if there is no resurrection of the dead, then Christ has not been raised; and if Christ has not been raised, then our proclamation is without foundation, and so is your faith. In addition, we are found to be false witnesses about God, because we have testified about God that He raised up Christ—whom He did not raise up if in fact the dead are not raised. For if the dead are not raised, Christ has not been raised. And if Christ has not been raised, your faith is worthless; you are still in your sins."

The apostles, who saw Jesus after his death and resurrection, clearly knew based on firsthand evidence that He was alive. Thus every one of them willingly died for Him because they knew the truth of His passion. In fact, His passion became their passion. Without this assurance, they would have scattered in many directions trying to save their own skin. Instead, they were martyred themselves, thus perpetuating the truth about Jesus Christ.

Years ago during my senior year of high school, I was impacted greatly by a sophomore on my football team. He understood and lived out the passion of Jesus Christ. When he practiced or played, he imagined Jesus Christ sitting in the bleachers watching his every move. His passion to perform for Jesus Christ was his only motivation. He gave effort which was beyond the entire team. I saw this young athlete work, sweat and compete for the glory of God. This sophomore's passion changed me and our entire team.

How about you? Are you willing to lay everything out on the field because Jesus Christ laid it all out for you? If so, your passion will impact people for eternity.

1. Read the crucifixion story found in the Gospels (Matthew 27-28 is one of the accounts). Discuss this event and why it was deemed important by the authorities to claim the body was stolen. Why the cover-up? Why is this story the most important historical event of all time?

2. What is something that you are passionate about? Why?

Passions can be very positive if directed correctly. You are warned in 2 Timothy 2:22 to flee from youthful passions, instead pursuing righteousness, faith, love and peace from a pure heart. When your passion is Christ-centered you will experience Him fully and completely. A relentless passionate pursuit of Christ will result in the abundant life He promises.

TOLERANCE

"But set apart the Messiah as Lord in your hearts, and always be ready to give a defense to anyone who asks you for a reason for the hope that is in you. However, do this with gentleness and respect, keeping your conscience clear... ." 1 Peter 3:15-16

In 2006, the Northwestern (IL) women's soccer team was suspended indefinitely after photographs of alleged hazing appeared on the Internet. The team issued an apology for the "negative attention, press and controversy" it caused the school. "We fully accept responsibility for our behavior and understand the magnitude and severity of the current situation," the team said in a letter that appeared in the school newspaper. They went on to say, "this incident does not reflect the values, integrity and qualities we seek to embody. We never foresaw that what began as a well-intentioned night of team unity and celebration would have such severe consequences."

Tolerance: Learning to accept others as valuable individuals regardless of their maturity.

1. Hazing and other acts of immaturity can have harmful consequences on individuals and teams. What are some consequences which occur when tolerance isn't exhibited?

Team Builder: Throw a team party void of alcohol, drugs, hazing and any other acts which could cause an incident affecting individual players, your school or community. After the party, discuss how everyone felt about exhibiting tolerance.

We live in a society which strives to be "politically correct." There are certain words and phrases which can't be used for fear of how people will react and respond. Today, I want to ask you a question, "Is Christianity tolerant?" The answer is, "Yes and no." How is that for being "politically correct"? Let me explain:

NO - Jesus himself was intolerant. He clearly tells us in John 14:6 that He is the way, the truth and the life and no one can come to the Father except through Him. In Acts 4:12 we are told there is no other name under heaven other than Jesus by which a person can be forgiven of his sins. It is intolerant to say there is only one true God as Jesus said in John 17:3. Jesus was intolerant when He said He is the one who reveals God to people (Luke 10:22). Jesus was extremely intolerant of religious hypocrisy when He condemned the religious know-it-alls, calling them deceivers (Matthew 23:25-26). Jesus was intolerant when He threw the moneychangers out of the Temple (John 2:13-16). Jesus was also intolerant of hatred (Luke 6:27), ignorance (Matthew 5) and prejudice (Luke 10:30-37).

In addition, Christianity is intolerant of serving false gods and false prophets. Christianity is intolerant because its founder, Jesus, was intolerant.

YES - Christianity is also tolerant. It teaches forgiveness (Matthew 18:21-22), patience and kindness (Galatians 5:22-23) and honesty and wholesomeness (Philippians 4:6-8). Jesus taught us to love and to be examples of truth to the world. While he was intolerant of pride, rebellion, sin, covetousness, adultery, lying, cheating, stealing, fornicating and murder, yet at the same time He demonstrated great love and patience with those who were guilty of all these things. God's intolerance for sin does not negate His love for people. God desires to help us avoid sin fleeing from temptations, bringing about holiness, peace and righteousness in our lives (Hebrews 12:10-11).

The fact of the matter is we are all sinners and the payment for sin is death and separation from God (Romans 3:23; 6:23). Jesus died to pay the penalty in full for our sins. Romans 5:8 reminds us that while we were yet sinners, Christ died for us. Because He died to pay for our sins, we can have a relationship with God.

1. How do you view Christianity relating to tolerance and intolerance?

2. How can Christians show more tolerance and yet not be guilty of violating God's truth?

3. How tolerant are you personally?

The issue of whether or not Christianity is tolerant lies in who Jesus is, what He claimed, and what He did. If what Jesus said and did is true, then Christianity is both tolerant and intolerant. Christ's message boils down to the truth of His life.

It is true Jesus lived. It is true Jesus walked on water (Matthew 8:26-27). It is true Jesus healed the sick (Matthew 8:5-13). It is true Jesus calmed a storm with a command (Mark 4:39). It is true Jesus raised the dead (Matthew 9:25; John 11:43-44). It is true Jesus claimed to be God (John 5:18; 8:24; 8:58—see Exodus 3:14). It is true Jesus was killed on a cross (Luke 24:20). It is true Jesus rose from the dead (Luke 24:39). It is true doubting Thomas became believing Thomas when he put his hands into the nail pierced hands of Jesus (John 20:24-28). It is true over 500 eyewitnesses saw Jesus (1 Corinthians 15:4-6) before He ascended into heaven (Acts 1:9-11). It is true the disciples who hid themselves and denied Jesus when He was arrested prior to His crucifixion became martyrs. In fact, Peter insisted on being crucified upside down on a cross at his death.

These are not feeble claims made by crazy people who wanted to gain power and fame. These are the truths of Christ and of those who followed Him, suffered for Him, and died for Him.

Either Christianity is wholly true or it is not. Either Jesus performed miracles or He did not. Either Jesus rose from the dead or He did not. Based solely and completely on who Jesus is and what He did, Christianity is the truth and by necessity all other religions that disagree with Jesus are wrong. If Christianity is false, then Jesus was not God and everything He said and did is a total fraud. But, if He is who He claims, then Christianity alone is true.

So how does your team practice tolerance? I encourage you to speak the truth in love by being real and caring. Being antagonistic, prideful, manipulative and telling people they are going to hell isn't a way to communicate God's love. Be intolerant of the world's view of God and values. Cling to your faith and don't give in. However, like Christ, you can be intolerant but also tolerant at the same time without compromising godly standards including honesty, responsibility, thoughtfulness, punctuality, self-control, patience, purity, compassion, diligence, etc. May your response to others be in line with today's memory verse.

1. Look up all the Scripture noted in this lesson (there's a ton of it). Was Jesus a liar, a lunatic or the Lord?

2. How can I stand my ground for my beliefs, yet minister effectively to those around me?

We are admonished in Scripture to always be ready to give a defense to anyone who asks for a reason for the hope which is inside us. This should be done with gentleness and respect, with a clear conscience (1 Peter 3:15-16). Living tolerantly can be challenging especially when it involves deep convictions. Therefore, fix your eyes on Christ and ask Him for help when opportunities emerge.

VISIONARY

"Without revelation (vision) people run wild, but one who keeps the law will be happy." Proverbs 29:18

At 5-foot-6 and 165 pounds, his chances of playing football for Notre Dame were slim to none. But Rudy Ruettiger had envisioned himself playing for the Fighting Irish since he was a boy, and he was willing to pay the price to make it happen. In 1974 he walked on and made the practice squad, and in 1975 got to dress for the final home game of his senior season. In Ruettiger's last opportunity to play for Notre Dame, Coach Dan Devine put Rudy into the game against Georgia Tech. In the movie Rudy, Devine is given a somewhat antagonistic role, not wanting Rudy to dress for his last game. However, in actuality, it was Devine who came up with the idea to dress Rudy. Ruettiger actually played for three plays.

The first play was a kickoff, the second play was an incomplete pass, and the third (and final) play of the game he sacked the quarterback. Ruettiger was carried off the field by his teammates, the first of only two players in Notre Dame history to have this honor.

Visionary: Dreaming not inhibited by the unknown. Looking beyond problems by creating successful solutions.

1. What are your dreams and aspirations for sports and life in general?

2. What are you doing today to help pave the way for your vision?

Team Builder: Rent the movie "Rudy" and watch it with your team. Talk about the vision he had and how his determination to see that vision come true resulted in an amazing story.

Rudy says, "Along the way the journey will be full of struggle, but I learned that the greater the struggle, the greater the victory!"

I have heard that 90 percent of all millionaires have a personal mission or vision statement, yet fewer than three percent of all other individuals have one. A vision statement helps people discover what drives them, where their passions lie and what brings energy and focus. It is a compass or a road map with a plan for lifelong learning and personal development. It needs to be continually prayed through and evaluated.

One practical step you can take as an individual or a team is to develop a vision statement. The most effective statements are one sentence long, can be understood by a 12-year-old and can be recited at gunpoint. After this statement is prepared, you can develop a series of goals to establish a thorough game plan. This will help give you direction, purpose and focus on what is really important.

God has uniquely gifted you with the personality, talent and experience to accomplish more than you can even dream or imagine (Ephesians 3:20). Today, let us understand that we must act on our God-given vision. Author and pastor Andy Stanley reminds us, "If God has birthed a vision in your heart, the day will come when you will be called upon to make a sacrifice to achieve it. And you will have to make the sacrifice with no guarantee of success." We know that the sowing of great sacrifices is required for the reaping of great rewards.

Stanley puts it this way: "Vision requires the commitment of a parachutist. You don't 'sort of' parachute. You are either in the plane or in the air." I challenge you to take the risks and make the sacrifices needed in order to move toward the vision God has put in your heart.

Caleb was an example of a man who had a vision statement. In Joshua 14:6-12, at the ripe age of 85 he still had a clear vision, an incredible passion and was ready to take action. He exclaimed, "I want this hill!" The fire was still burning in him as he continued to trust and believe in God.

1. Do you have a personal mission or vision statement? If so, share it with your team. If not, commit to creating one prior to your next meeting.

2. Does your team have a vision statement? If so, review your statement and talk about what it means to each person. If you don't have a team statement, work together on establishing one and then identify specific goals which will help you achieve the vision statement.

3. Do a Bible search on Caleb and read the various stories on his life. Why was his phrase "I want this hill" so important to him?

 WRAPUP

Years ago, I heard former professional baseball player and current MLB analyst, Harold Reynolds speak on "vision" and he shared several important truths including:

* Have a vision: Habakkuk 2:2 says to write your vision down, so you'll recognize it when it unfolds. We have to know our reason for living.

* Commit to the vision: Just like focusing a camera, making a commitment helps focus our vision, making it clearer to us. It helps to begin with the end in mind which allows us to see the outcome before others do.

* Don't get distracted or discouraged from the vision. Jesus came so we could have life, but Satan wants to steal, kill and destroy (John 10:10).

* Stay on the right path because it builds confidence. Proverbs 4:18 says, "The path of the righteous is like the first gleam of dawn, shining ever brighter till the full light of day." The further you go, the clearer things will get.

* Allow the vision to mature. Sometimes we give up too fast. It takes nine months for a baby to develop and mature within the womb before it is born. As Christians, we need to have patience in our spiritual growth. Growth takes time. We should remember this when we bring

people to Christ. We must provide for follow-up, not just say, "I'm glad you've made a commitment. Now grow up." Visions take time.

* Develop good work habits. Excellence in any area of life demands good work habits...whether prayer, Bible reading or baseball. I worked on my swing and developed good habits in baseball, and even though I still have rough times, those good baseball habits will get me through.

* Run through the tape. You have all seen sprinters lean into the tape at the end of the race. In the spiritual race of life it's not how well you start but who endures to the end and leans to the tape (1 Corinthians 9:24-25).

* Remember the vision because the vision keeps you alive. Proverbs 29:18 reminds us that when there is no vision, we perish.

The process of writing a vision statement and establishing goals can be one of the most valuable exercises you will ever go through. Try it.

1. Review the following passages (Genesis 12:1-5; Mark 1:16-20; Mark 2:1-5 and 2 Corinthians 11:16-27) and discuss the risks and sacrifices required.

2. Review the list of items mentioned by Harold Reynolds and comment on each statement.

3. Reflect on the vision God has currently put on your heart. What sacrifices are necessary? Are you willing to make them?

4. What types of customs, traditions and attitudes do you want to pass on to your future children and grandchildren?

A visionary person is able to look optimistically ahead and not be deterred by potential obstacles. I encourage you to relentlessly dream big dreams. Ask God to solidify your vision. Articulate your vision to others and invite them to join you on the journey. Prayerfully review the truth statements shared by Harold Reynolds if you get discouraged along the way.

WORSHIP

DOING IT IN SPIRIT AND TRUTH

"God is spirit, and those who worship Him must worship in spirit and truth." John 4:24

At the 1924 Paris Olympics, Eric Liddell dropped out of his best event, the 100-yard dash, because qualifying heats were held on a Sunday. Instead, Liddell entered himself in the 400-yard dash. During the Sunday heats, he preached a sermon at a Paris church. The 400-yard dash was not what he had trained for, but Liddell finished five yards ahead of his nearest competitor, setting a world record of 47.6 seconds. He attributed his win to God. Eric stated, "The secret of my success over the 400 metres is that I run the first 200 metres as hard as I can. Then, for the second 200 metres, with God's help, I run harder." After his triumph at the Olympics, Liddell moved to China as a missionary, following in his parents' footsteps. The critically-acclaimed and Oscar winning 1981 film, Chariots of Fire, is based in part on the story of Eric Liddell.

Worship: Honoring God reverently.

1. Where do you go to worship the Lord?

2. How would you define worship? How do you worship?

3. Is it possible to worship God while competing in a sport? Why or why not?

Team Builder: Do a google search on Eric Liddell and discover the depth of his story and his character. Discuss as a team ways you can worship the Lord.

Eric Liddell was a man who totally surrendered his life to God (James 4:7). He was willing to accept anything God did in his life whether it was running through the tape on the race track or serving in China. This is true worship!!

In contrast to Eric's lifestyle of worship, we don't often see this example in the real world. As you read the story in the WRAPUP section, consider how this ties to worship. Is worship confined to a building or a structure? Is it possible to worship God Almighty anywhere, anytime, anyplace? Several memorable quotes from Eric Liddell are noted in Chariots of Fire. In one scene, Eric says, "Then where does the power come from, to see the race to its end? From within." Later he says, "I believe God made me for a purpose, but he also made me fast. And when I run I feel His pleasure." Eric Liddell worshipped God through his sport and later he worshipped the Lord by serving as a missionary until his death.

According to one pastor, "The heart of worship is surrender. In today's culture we are taught to never give up and never give in-so we don't hear much about surrendering. If winning is everything, then surrendering is unthinkable." But surrendering to God, which brings God pleasure, happens when you give yourself completely to Him. It means giving God all of your life-sports, academics, relationships, career, etc. Surrendering to God is not being passive or lazy. It isn't suppressing your personality. C.S. Lewis said, "The more we let God take us over, the more truly ourselves we become-because he made us."

You know you are surrendered to God when you rely on Him to work things out as opposed to manipulating others, forcing your agenda or controlling situations. As Joshua approached the biggest battle of his life (Joshua 5:13-15), he encountered God, fell in worship before Him, and surrendered his plans. That surrender led to a stunning victory in Jericho. This is the paradox: Victory comes through surrender. Surrender doesn't weaken you; it strengthens you.

1. How do you view the words "surrender" and "winning"? Can they occur simultaneously? How can you surrender to win in your life?

2. Based on the information above, what is your view of worship?

3. How do your actions in practice and on game day compare to your actions during worship?

WRAPUP

The world championship hung in the balance when Briana Scurry, the American goalkeeper, strode to the goal line at the Women's World Cup. Scurry had picked out her victim, the third Chinese player to take a penalty kick in the shootout.....it was one thing to choose which opponent was most likely to be weak. It was another thing for Scurry to choose her tactics. By her own admission, Scurry decided to improve her chances by ignoring the penalty kick rules. In a quick and practiced move, Scurry bolted two steps forward-a violation-and cut off the angle for Liu Ying, her opponent. With superb reflexes, Scurry then dove to her left and tipped Liu's shot wide of the goal. That one stop gave the U.S. the championship. Scurry's position was clear soon after the game when she told The *Los Angeles Times:* "Everybody does it. It's only cheating if you get caught."

The lessons you have read throughout this book have all prepared you for this final chapter on worship. To worship is to "honor God reverently." He is the object of our worship. He makes it worth it all. Our one goal in life should be to worship Him and to bring Him glory, honor and praise. He demands it, and He deserves it. The Brianna Scurry story is a smack in the face of worship. Is life all about trying to gain a competitive edge, winking at sin when you don't get caught? The reality is that we all will stand before God someday and give a full accounting of our life to Him. (see Ecclesiastes 12:13-14 for maybe the most terrifying and sobering verse in all of Scripture).

He should be our only audience. We should view our lives as an opportunity to worship Him alone. My encouragement to you is to worship Him in spirit and in truth (John 4:24). Perform solely for Him. Use your God-given talents to bring Him glory. Sink deep into His Word and let Him guide you.

1. Reflect on the words of Jonathan Edwards who said, "I claim no right to myself—no right to understand, this will and these affections that are in me; neither do I have any right to this body or its members—any right to this tongue, to these hands, feet, ears, of my own. To God this morning I have given myself wholly—I purpose to be absolutely His." What does this statement tell you about the way Jonathan worshipped?

2. Describe what it means to play to an "Audience of One." Refer to Colossians 3:17 and 23.

3. Read Psalm 33 and 98. How do these chapters exhort us to worship?

Our goal should be to worship Him in spirit and in truth (John 4:24). Worshipping God can only be done through the One (Jesus) who bridged the gap between a holy God and us. This type of worship pleases God immensely because worship goes to the core of who we are as a person. Be relentless in your worship. He is your only true Audience. He glories in having this relationship with you.

FCA

FELLOWSHIP OF CHRISTIAN ATHLETES

Getting Involved With FCA

Since 1954, the Fellowship of Christian Athletes has challenged athletes and coaches to impact the world for Jesus Christ. FCA is cultivating Christian principles in local communities nationwide by encouraging, equipping and empowering others to serve as examples and make a difference. Reaching approximately two million people annually on the professional, college, high school, junior high and youth levels, FCA has grown into the largest Christian sports ministry in the world. Through FCA's Four Cs of Ministry—Coaches, Campus, Camps and Community—and the shared passion for athletics and faith, lives are changed for current and future generations.

FCA'S FOUR Cs OF MINISTRY

Coaches: Coaches are the heart of FCA. Our role is to minister to them by encouraging and equipping them to know and serve Christ. FCA ministers to coaches through Bible studies, prayer support, discipleship and mentoring, resources, outreach events and retreats. FCA values coaches, first for who they are, and also for what God has created them to do.

Campus: The Campus Ministry is initiated and led by student athletes and coaches on junior high, high school, and college campuses. The Campus Ministry types—Huddles, Team Bible Studies, Chaplain Programs and Coaches Bible Studies—are effective ways to establish FCA ministry presence, as well as outreach events such as One Way 2 Play—Drug Free programs, school assemblies and Fields of Faith.

Camp: Camp is a time of "inspiration and perspiration" for coaches and athletes to reach their potential by offering comprehensive athletic, spiritual and leadership training. FCA offers seven types of camps: Sports Camps, Leadership Camps, Coaches Camps, Power Camps, Partnership Camps, Team Camps and International Camps.

Community: FCA has ministries that reach the community through partnerships with local churches, businesses, parents and volunteers. These ministries not only reach out to the community, but also allow the community to invest in athletes and coaches. Non school-based sports, adult ministries, youth sports, FCA Teams, clinics, resources and professional athlete ministries are the areas of Community Ministry.

VISION
To see the world impacted for Jesus Christ through the influence of coaches and athletes.

FCACampus101.com   FCAResources.com   facebook.com/FCAfans

twitter.com/fcanews   FCA.org   r12coach.com

Fellowship of Christian Athletes
8701 Leeds Road • Kansas City, MO 64129
www.fca.org • fca@fca.org • 1-800-289-0909
COMPETITORS FOR CHRIST

More Than WINNING

Your Game Plan for Life.

GOD'S PLAN

In most athletic contests a coach prepares a game plan ahead of time. God designed a plan for our lives before the world began.

God is holy and perfect. He created us to love Him, glorify Him, and enjoy Him forever.

WHAT IS GOD'S STANDARD?

The Bible, God's playbook, says that the standard for being on His team is to:

Be holy.
"Be holy because I am holy."-1 Peter 1:16

Be perfect.
"Be perfect, therefore, as your heavenly Father is perfect."-Matthew 5:48

WHAT IS GOD'S PLAN?

God created us to:

Love Him.
"He said to him, 'Love the Lord your God with all your heart, with all your soul, and with all your mind.'"-Matthew 22:37

Glorify (honor) Him.
"Our Lord and God, You are worthy to receive glory and honor and power, because You have created all things, and because of Your will they exist and were created."-Revelation 4:11

Enjoy Him forever.
Jesus said, *"...I have come that they may have life and have it in abundance."*
　　　　　　　　　　　　-John 10:10

Why is it that we cannot live up to God's standard of holiness and perfection and fulfill God's plan for our lives?
Because of...

MAN'S PROBLEM

Man is sinful and is separated from God.

WHAT IS SIN?

Sin means missing the mark, falling short of God's standard. It is not only doing wrong and failing to do what God wants (lying, gossip, losing our temper, lustful thoughts, etc.), but it is also an attitude of ignoring or rejecting God which is a result of our sinful nature.

"Indeed, I was guilty [when I] was born..."
　　　　　　　　　　　　-Psalm 51:5

WHO HAS SINNED?

"For all have sinned and fall short of the glory of God."-Romans 3:23

WHAT'S THE RESULT OF SIN?

Separation from God.
"But your iniquities have built barriers between you and your God..."-Isaiah 59:2

Death.
"For the wages of sin is death..."
-Romans 6:23

Judgment.
"...just as it is appointed for people to die once—and after this, judgment"
-Hebrews 9:27

This illustration shows that God is holy and we are sinful and separated from Him. Man continually tries to reach God through his own efforts (being good, religious activities, philosophy, etc.) but, while these can be good things, they all fall short of God's standard.

"All of us have become like something unclean, and all our righteous acts are like a polluted garment..."-Isaiah 64:6

There is only one way to bridge this gap between God and man...

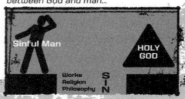

GOD'S SUBSTITUTE

God provided the only way to be on His team by sending His son, Jesus Christ, as the holy and perfect substitute to die in our place.

WHO IS JESUS CHRIST?

He is God.
Jesus said, *"The Father and I are one."*
-John 10:30

He is Man.
"...the Word (Jesus) was God...The Word became flesh and took up residence among us."-John 1:1,14

WHAT HAS JESUS DONE?

He died as our substitute.
"God proves His own love for us in that while we were still sinners Christ died for us!"-Romans 5:8

He rose from the dead.
"...Christ died for our sins..He was buried...He was raised on the third day according to the Scriptures and...He appeared to Cephas, then to the Twelve. Then He appeared to over 500 brothers at one time..."-1 Corinthians 15:3-6

He is the only way to God.
"I am the way, the truth, and the life. No one comes to the Father except through Me."-John 14:6

This diagram shows that God has bridged the gap between Himself and man by sending Jesus Christ to die in our place as our substitute. Jesus defeated sin and death and rose from the grave. Yet, it isn't enough just to know these facts. *The following page tells how to become part of God's team and experience His plan...*

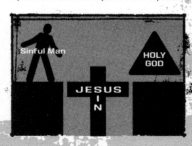

MAN'S RESPONSE

Knowing a lot about a sport and "talking the game" doesn't make you a member of a team. The same is true in becoming a Christian. It takes more than just knowing about Jesus Christ; it requires a total commitment by faith in Him.

FAITH IS NOT:

Just knowing the facts.
"You believe that God is one; you do well. The demons also believe—and they shudder."-James 2:19

Just an emotional experience.
Raising your hand or repeating a prayer is not enough.

 FAITH IS:

Repenting.
Turning to God from sin.
"For godly grief produces a repentance not to be regretted and leading to salvation..."
                    -2 Corinthians 7:10

Receiving Jesus Christ.
Trusting in Christ alone for salvation.
"But to all who did receive Him, He gave them the right to be children of God, to those who believe in His name..."
                    -John 1:12

Look at the diagram-
On which side do you see yourself? Where would you like to be?

Jesus said, *"I assure you: Anyone who hears My word and believes Him who sent Me has eternal life and will not come under judgment but has passed from death to life."*-John 5:24

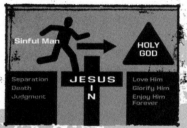

REPLAY OF GOD'S PLAN

 REalize God is holy and perfect; we are sinners and cannot save ourselves.

 REcognize who Jesus is and what He's done as our substitute.

 REceive Jesus Christ by faith as Savior and Lord.
"But to all who did receive Him, He gave them the right to become children of God, to those who believe in His name..."-John 1:12, 13

REspond to Jesus Christ in a life of obedience.
"If anyone wants to come with me, he must deny himself, take up his cross daily, and follow Me."-Jesus, Luke 9:23

Does God's plan make sense to you? Are you willing to repent and receive Jesus Christ?

If so, express to God your need for him. Consider the "Suggested Prayer of Surrender" on the next page. Remember that God is more concerned with your attitude than with the words you say.

PRAYER OF SURRENDER

> "Lord Jesus, I need you. I realize I'm a sinner, and I can't save myself. I need Your forgiveness. I believe that You loved me so much that You died on the cross for my sins and rose from the dead. I repent of my sins and put my faith in You as Savior and Lord. Today, I surrender my life. I am all in, Jesus. Take control of my life and help me to follow You in obedience. I love You, Jesus. In Jesus' name, Amen."

"...If you confess with your mouth, 'Jesus is Lord', and believe in your heart that God raised Him from the dead, you will be saved...for 'Everyone who calls on the name of the Lord will be saved'"
—Romans 10:9,13

Once you have committed your life to Jesus Christ, it is important to understand what your position is on this team...

KNOW YOUR POSITION

Too many people make the mistake of measuring the certainty of their salvation by their feelings instead of the facts of God's Word. In Jesus Christ you have a new life. See what God's Word says about your new position on His team...

N I am a New Creation in Christ.
2 Corinthians 5:17; Galatians 2:20

E I have Everything I need for life and godliness.
2 Peter 1:3; Ephesians 1:3

W I am a Witness for Christ and am His Workmanship, created for good works.
Acts 1:8; Ephesians 2:10

L I am Loved and accepted completely in Christ.
Ephesians 1:6; Romans 8:39

I I am Indwelt by the Holy Spirit.
1 Corinthians 6:19, 20; 1 John 4:4

F I am Forgiven and Free from condemnation.
1 John 1:9; Romans 8:1-2

E I have Eternal Life in Christ.
John 5:24; 1 John 5:11-13

Trust God! Put your faith in His Word, not in your feelings: *"I have written these things to you who believe in the name of the Son of God, so that you may know that you have eternal life."*
-1 John 5:13

4 DAILY EXERCISES

Just as physical growth demands physical exercise, spiritual growth as a Christian demands spiritual exercise. To build spiritual muscle here are four daily exercises.

1. Daily Seek Christ.

Spend time every day reading God's Word and devoting time in prayer.

"...they welcomed the message with eagerness and examined the Scriptures daily to see if these things were so."-Acts 17:11

"I praise You seven times a day..."-Psalm 119:164

2. Daily Share Christ.

Share Jesus every day through your words and actions.

"Every day in the temple complex, and in various homes, they continued teaching and proclaiming the good news that the Messiah is Jesus."
-Acts 5:42

"Therefore, we are ambassadors for Christ; certain that God is appealing through us..."
-2 Corinthians 5:20

3. Daily Lead Others.

Lead others by serving as Christ did. Every day die to self and yield complete control of your life to Jesus Christ.

"The greatest among you will be your servant."
-Matt 23:11

"If anyone wants to come with Me, he must deny himself, take up his cross daily, and follow Me."
-Luke 9:23

4. Daily Love Others.

Take every opportunity to show others around you that you love them.

"...love your neighbor as yourself..."-Mark 12:33

"But encourage each other daily, while it is still called today..."-Heb 3:13

Do these exercises and you will grow strong in your Christian life and be an effective member of God's team.

If you made a commitment to Christ, or rededicated your life to Christ, FCA wants to know. Please do one of the following so we can help you:

 1. Log on to www.morethanwinning.org and record your decision.

2. Contact us at 1-800-289-0909 or fca@fca.org.

3. Contact your local FCA office.

FELLOWSHIP OF CHRISTIAN ATHLETES

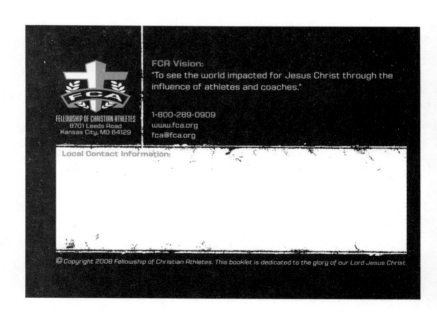

FELLOWSHIP OF CHRISTIAN ATHLETES
8701 Leeds Road
Kansas City, MO 64129

FCA Vision:
"To see the world impacted for Jesus Christ through the influence of athletes and coaches."

1-800-289-0909
www.fca.org
fca@fca.org

Local Contact Information:

Team Character Survey – Character Attributes

This survey is intended to help you and your team assess personal and team character attributes. The results can be analyzed by you individually for your personal growth, but analyzing your team's collective responses can also provide an overview of the areas where your team is strong and areas for character growth.

INSTRUCTIONS: For each item below, circle the number that most closely reflects your personal sense of the strength or weakness of the given character attribute in your own life.

SCALE

1	2	3	4	5	6	7	8	9	10
WEAK									**STRONG**

1. **Love:** I easily develop deep personal attachments and affections for other people.

1   2   3   4   5   6   7   8   9   10

2. **Devotion:** I am earnestly and enthusiastically committed to pursuing things of great value.

1   2   3   4   5   6   7   8   9   10

3. **Freedom:** I am currently experiencing total unrestraint from all areas of bondage.

1   2   3   4   5   6   7   8   9   10

4. **Mission:** I have the ability to share my life experiences with all kinds of people.

1   2   3   4   5   6   7   8   9   10

5. **Accountability:** I am regularly answerable to God and at least one other person for my behavior.

1   2   3   4   5   6   7   8   9   10

6. **Cheerful:** It is in my nature to express encouragement, approval or congratulations at the proper time.

1   2   3   4   5   6   7   8   9   10

7. **Compassion:** I frequently invest my time, talents, treasures or whatever else is necessary to heal the hurts of others by a willingness to bear their pain.

1   2   3   4   5   6   7   8   9   10

8. **Determination:** I am able work intently to accomplish goals regardless of the opposition.

1   2   3   4   5   6   7   8   9   10

9. **Enthusiasm:** I often express lively, absorbing interest in each task as I give it my best effort.

1   2   3   4   5   6   7   8   9   10

10. **Faith:** I have an unshakable confidence in God, with actions that prove it.

1   2   3   4   5   6   7   8   9   10

11. **Forgiveness:** I am able to clear the record of those who have wronged me and not hold their past offenses against them.

1   2   3   4   5   6   7   8   9   10

12. **Obedience:** I regularly fulfill instructions so the one I am serving is fully satisfied and pleased.

1   2   3   4   5   6   7   8   9   10

13. **Passionate:** I often have intense, powerful or compelling emotions and feelings towards others or something.

1   2   3   4   5   6   7   8   9   10

14. **Tolerance:** I am learning to accept others as valuable individuals regardless of their maturity.

1   2   3   4   5   6   7   8   9   10

15. **Visionary:** My dreams are not inhibited by the unknown. I am able to look beyond problems by creating successful solutions.

1   2   3   4   5   6   7   8   9   10

16. **Worship:** It is my desire to honor God reverently.

1   2   3   4   5   6   7   8   9   10

Summary Question:
Besides physical abilities, what do you believe are the three most important ingredients this team needs to be highly successful?

1. Absolutely Mission-Critical: _____
2. Very Important: _____
3. Important: _____
Name _____ (optional)

Practice Evaluation

The "practice evaluation" form is an accountability tool utilized by the coach(es) to reinforce key principles and strategies utilized by the team. The example shown below is based upon one used by Nebraska's Head Volleyball Coach John Cook. Ideally, the coaches and players will work together prior to the season to design a form resulting in buy-in from the entire team. The team, working in conjunction with the coaching staff, can modify the principles to suit your own emphasis areas. In this example, this team is enforcing six character development areas for every single practice. At the end of each practice, each player does a self-evaluation and turns it into the coaching staff. The player will give a numerical rating (1-5) on the six different categories and then have an opportunity to write a brief statement addressing any area of concern. This evaluation can be done via a text, email or a hard copy. The results are reviewed daily by the coaching staff and appropriate action is taken to correct shortfalls. The benefits include, increased communication, high accountability, character development, etc.

One coach uses this tool at halftime of the games by having players pair up and give a quick 30-second briefing to a teammate. Another coach uses these principles as talking points before, during and after games as opposed to just sharing statistical information. We encourage you to utilize this form "as is" or modify it to suit your team's desire.

Practice Evaluation Form

Rating Scale 1 = Failing
2 = Poor
3 = Average
4 = Good Job
5 = Excellent

Develops Championship Habits	☐	Servant Leadership	☐
Maximum Effort	☐	Make Players Around You Better	☐
Communication	☐	Trusts Coaches and Respects Them	☐

Total ☐

Text/email coach after every practice or game with your score

-Comments on situations in practice
-How you responded
-Explain a better way to respond   Initial ☐

_____
_____
_____